He's Gone
Now What?

*How to Get Over a Breakup
and Prepare to Love Again*

Gregg Michaelsen

DISCLAIMER:

As a male dating coach I am very good at what I do because of my years of studying the nuances of interpersonal relationships. I have helped thousands of women understand men. That said, I am not a psychologist, doctor or licensed professional. So do not use my advice as a substitute if you need professional help.

Women tell me how much I have helped them and I truly hope that I can HELP you too in your pursuit of that extraordinary man! I will provide you with powerful tools. YOU need to bring me your willingness to listen and CHANGE!

———————————————

Table of Contents

Introduction

Getting over a painful experience is much like crossing monkey bars.
You have to let go at some point in order to move forward.
~C. S. Lewis~

You are in what feels like the worst phase of your life. You were in what you thought was a happy, successful relationship and then the rug was pulled from beneath you and now you feel like you're free-falling. You're questioning everything, mostly yourself. Your friends and family are all sympathetic and are probably walking on eggshells around you, afraid to set off the waterworks.

Meanwhile, you're trying to figure out where things went wrong. You're probably beating yourself up, perhaps with the help of your ex if he feels the need to tell you every flaw he ever saw in you. Many men won't do this – it's mostly a thing women do – but some men will if they're also hurting or their confidence is in the tank.

Breakups are terrible, and they do their own kind of damage on your confidence and self-esteem. In most of my books, I am trying to help you learn how to attract or keep a man and confidence always plays a role in that process but you're in a different place.

Your knee-jerk reaction might be to get right back out there and find another guy but I am going to ask you to hold off on that process for a while – at least until you read this book!

Why?

I know. Your friends and family are telling you to get back on the horse – not to be afraid – to forget that jerk and find a great guy. I agree with all of that, but I don't agree with the timing. So much is going on in your mind and body right now that processing a new relationship would not end well.

Before you can get back out there, you need to process the breakup. There are many things going on in your mind and body right now that you need to address. As we are about to discover, both your mind and your body are impacted by a breakup in ways you can't even imagine. Those effects are causing you to react to things in certain, sometimes counterproductive ways.

This book is split into three phases. Phase 1 explains to you everything that's going on in your mind and body and helps you understand the strategies you need to counter these things. Phase 2 takes you through the process of healing from the breakup. You'll find strategies for proceeding through your pain into a healthier, more independent and ready for a relationship you. In Phase 3, you are going to learn about moving forward. We're going to examine a few topics of importance like where happiness comes from, setting boundaries and how to know when you're really in love, just to name a few.

This is your time, while you are single, to pull yourself back together into a stronger, confident woman who chooses great men. Gone are the days of being grateful to be chosen by a man who turns out to be a loser.

Rest assured, I plan to take it slow, but I am your coach and I am going to push you, just a bit at times, to become the best version of you possible! Are you ready?

As part of your healing process, I would like to offer you a free copy of my book, Own Your Tomorrow. *While you're not in a place to read it today, you will be soon and I want you to have it when you need it! Email me at* Gregg@WhoHoldsTheCardsNow.com *and put* ICAN *in the subject line. I will email the free book to you as soon as I can. Please give me a day to do so. A review of this book, or any of my books is always welcome.*

PHASE 1
What Happens to Your Mind and Body When You Break Up?

I don't know how long ago your breakup occurred or whether it was your idea or his, but what I do know is that there are some definite things which happen in your mind and body – things which really toy with you and make you think you're losing your mind – rest assured, you're not, but let's first spend some time examining what happens to these two areas of your life.

Chapter 1

How Your Body Reacts to a Break Up

I'll bet you didn't know that there are scientifically proven physiological responses to a breakup. Not only does your body react to a breakup, but it does so in a big way. Science (Fisher 2004) tells us that your body goes through a legitimate withdrawal process after a breakup.

Chemical Reactions

When you are happy and in love, you are producing higher than normal amounts of what we can call happy neurotransmitters: dopamine, oxytocin and serotonin. The research I just mentioned, conducted by my friend, Helen Fisher, indicates that recovering from this withdrawal is more difficult than withdrawal from a cocaine addiction – those chemicals are that powerful in your body.

When you suffer withdrawal from these chemicals, you feel physical pain more intensely and you may seek out activities which boost your dopamine levels, like binge eating, shopping or becoming sexually promiscuous. Without knowing why you're doing those things, you still may engage in them because they make you feel better, even if temporarily.

Instead of binge eating, you could lose your appetite, which could indicate that you've slid into a depression. You may also have many restless or sleepless nights. This often happens when you're fixating on the happy moments of the relationship or the breakup itself.

It is important for me to stop here and say one critical thing. If you feel extremely depressed – you can't get out of bed, you can't stop crying or you just feel terribly down in the dumps, you need to seek professional counseling. Reading a book is not going to be enough to help you. This book will help, but you can't focus on healing when your body is reacting in this way. If you feel suicidal, take yourself to an emergency room. They are equipped to help. Please, please seek the help you need.

Along with the breakup, you are probably feeling higher than normal levels of stress. This releases cortisol, a chemical responsible for, among other things, increasing your heart rate. Cortisol is knick-named the stress hormone and is one of your fight or flight chemicals. This chemical, when triggered in fight or flight mode, takes a few minutes to kick in, versus others which act in seconds. Still, the impact cannot be ignored.

Cortisol regulates your blood pressure, the levels of fluid in your body, your sex drive, your immune system, your digestive system and growth. Obviously, you're past a growth phase, but the remaining systems are all impacted when you feel the stress of a breakup.

While all of this can be useful if your fight or flight mechanism has kicked in, prolonged higher than normal levels of cortisol can be very detrimental to your health. Too much cortisol over a longer period of time can lead to obesity, decreased sex drive, a depleted immune system (you'll get sick more often), increased blood pressure and blood sugar levels and you can get a nice case of acne on top of all of that other misery.

Emotional Reactions

The longer the two of you were together, the more of your identity rests in being part of a couple. Your friends probably didn't say "you", they probably said "you guys" when they included you in an invitation or conversation. Now, you need to re-identify who you are, and this isn't just a language issue. When you are part of a couple, you may develop values as a couple that might not fit you any longer. Our values change when our lives change.

For example, maybe as a couple, you valued spending time together on Saturday mornings. Now what do you do with your Saturdays? You might replace valuing that together time with volunteering at a local shelter or working on yourself.

In addition to being part of a "we" for some period of time, you are now faced with the emotional trauma and physical challenge of letting go of the love you had for him. Even if you are the one who dumped him, you still loved him at some point and it is hard to let those feelings go. In order to avoid letting go of the happy chemicals, your mind is conspiring against you and is trying to hold onto those happy feelings.

Another problem you may face in becoming single again is that you had an emotional support system in your partner. You were able to lean on him when things got tough and he on you. If he had become your only support system, you may really be feeling despair right now. Who are you leaning on, now that you truly need support?

What Does It Mean?

All of this, summed up, means breakups are no joke. They are really hard on your physical and emotional systems. You have genuine physiological reactions to losing the love you felt for him and that, combined with the emotional reactions is leaving you in a tough spot. Your friends and family may be saying things like "You just need to move on" or asking, "Why can't you just let go of it?" Now you know why.

Throughout this book, we will continue to explore what your mind and body are going through so you have a better understanding of what you're feeling and how you can overcome those feelings.

What Can You Do?

What is important about this chapter, and why it is the first chapter of this book, is that you need to have a full understanding right away of what you're experiencing. You might think you're going crazy or that there is something seriously wrong with you. You may not recognize the physical responses you're having to the breakup as being associated with it, but now you can see that your desire to binge eat or your lack of appetite are both normal responses to your emotional pain. Stubbing your toe on the dresser did hurt more than usual because your chemicals are all out of whack and you're feeling pain more deeply than normal.

Acknowledge the addiction your brain has to the happy chemicals and the difficulty you will have in breaking that addiction. Know that you are in the beginning phases of feeling this way but there is an end in sight. Understand that you need to feel the pain, the anxiety and the heartbreak because the only way to stop feeling it is to first feel it and move through it.

When friends and family begin to encourage you to 'move on' or 'get over it', kindly tell them you are moving through this process at your pace, not theirs and thank them for their concern. Nobody can feel your pain for you and nobody knows what you're feeling today.

Right now, you might feel as if you'll never feel normal again. You'll never be over him, over the hurt. Feeling better seems to be impossible. I want you to hold onto that for just a moment while I tell you about impossible.

You can scour the Internet for hours and find dozens and dozens of stories of magnificent people overcoming daunting odds to achieve the impossible. I'll save you the time. The thing they all used, and the thing which is also available to you is an altered mindset. In every story you will read about someone achieving the impossible, the one common thread is a statement that goes something like this, "but they were unwilling to accept that their situation was impossible".

It is crucial for you to understand that your mindset, moving forward, is going to be what gets you through. You need to develop the resolve to push yourself through the difficult days. You need to experience a language change in your life. You need to learn to stop saying "I can't" and start saying "I can". "I can get through this". "I can love again". "I can feel this pain and be okay".

The biggest thing you can do for yourself before you continue reading is to adopt a mindset of "I can". Even if, right now, you don't really feel it, you need to begin saying it. Say it over and over to yourself as many times as it takes. When you hear "I can't", jump in there with "I can!!!" I know you might not believe any of this today and you may doubt that this will work for you, but what do you have to lose? Pain, anguish, despair? Sounds good to me!

Survival Tactic #1

Find a piece of paper and some markers, crayons or even a pencil. In letters as big as the space allows, write "I CAN". It doesn't have to be fancy but it needs to be as big as you can make it. Hang it up where you will see it often. You might need to make more than one of these signs. Do whatever it takes. "I can" applies not only to surviving this breakup, but it applies to all areas of your life. You can finish your education. You can get that promotion. You can run a mile, then two. You can feel pain and be okay. Your first survival tactic is simply to believe in yourself. With each day, you will find this belief to get a little stronger and there are some days you will slide backwards. That's why you have the signs – as a constant reminder that even though your mind might still be saying you can't, you know you can!

Chapter 2

Why Breakups Suck
SO Much

Whether you initiated the breakup or he did, breakups suck. There's just no other way to say it. Even if you initiated the breakup, you did so because you felt the relationship had come to its end for some reason. Something came between you. This means you may be feeling some form of rejection.

We are hardwired to fear rejection. It's a primal feeling that goes way back into our history when we were communal. If you were rejected from the community, you lost your entire support system and you would most likely die. Being tossed out of the community meant no food, no shelter, nobody to help you. Obviously, if we lose our support system today, we aren't likely to die, but it can feel that bad at times.

As we just learned, our chemical systems are alerted when we experience a breakup. This can best be described as being addicted to love, and as I mentioned earlier, this addiction is very difficult to overcome. In addition to the impact we've already discussed, you are battling feelings of loss in ways you can't even imagine.

You had someone to do things with. When a friend had a party, you had an automatic date. On holidays, you had someone to celebrate with. You may have been able to share chores like doing the dishes or laundry. Now, those activities you once did together can seem insurmountable. You see the stack of dishes but because you always washed and he dried, you can't seem to get up the motivation to do them.

When you feel this way, get out your "I CAN" sign from Survival Tactic #1! You *can* do this!

Along with missing his contributions to your life, the withdrawal from the 'love addiction' often leaves you feeling worthless and inadequate. Friends and family, while meaning well, may be giving you some bad advice. People will tell you to 'push through' or stuff those emotions of anger, sadness and despair but I am going to suggest to you that you do something different.

Rather than ignore or try to stuff those emotions, feel them and allow them to pass. Get angry that he isn't there to do the dishes. Cry about it. Feeling those emotions and seeing yourself come out okay on the other side helps you move beyond that anger and sadness. When you stuff them, you don't deal with them and they just continue to exist and build.

When you are in the early stages of a breakup, it is often easier to look back to the past. You dwell on what you perceive to be your failures and inadequacies. While this may seem like you're identifying your flaws so you can fix them, what you're actually doing is remaining stuck in that past and allowing a negative inner voice to take over.

Not only does dwelling on the past force you to stay stuck there and focused on negatives, it also prevents you from seeing the possibility of a new relationship. While you're not ready for that yet, it is something you will want at some point.

Dwelling on the past can also cause you to begin thinking you're a failure when it comes to relationships. I hear this from the women I coach all the time. They feel they have had so many bad relationship experiences that they define themselves as failures in relationships. This not only puts a negative light on past relationships, but it gives you a feeling that a future successful relationship isn't possible either.

Often, we aren't aware of how all of this negative self-talk impacts our lives but we hear those stories over and over and at some point, our brain begins to believe them.

What Does It Mean?

You're going to be feeling things which make you uncomfortable. Some of them are okay to feel, like anger and sadness. What is important is to allow those feelings to pass and then to recognize that you were able to feel those things and be okay after. This will help keep your stress levels low and consequently your stress chemicals will be lower.

Additionally, you need to become mindful of the self-talk you're using. Be aware of words like failure, inadequate, unlovable, fat, ugly, etc. Those words do nothing to help you through this process and, in fact, serve to delay your healing. While it may seem productive to call out your own flaws, dwelling on them is not.

What Can You Do?

Often, what you experience right after a breakup can be some form of fear. You're afraid nobody else will ever love you. You may be afraid to stay in your home alone. You may be afraid to pump gas at night – something your ex always did for you. You might be afraid of the painful feelings you're experiencing. Regardless of where the fear comes from, fear causes your brain to respond and that response comes in the form of those chemicals we just talked about in the last chapter.

The best way to combat the fight or flight chemicals is to exercise. I know this makes you want to roll your eyes but it's true and there is science behind me telling you this. When you exercise, your body releases endorphins. Endorphins are the anti-fight-or-flight chemicals. They stomp on those other chemicals and help them dissipate.

Exercise also allows you to focus on yourself. If you have children, you've probably shifted into a mode where doing something for yourself is nearly unheard of. You've put yourself last long enough. During the course of this book, I'm going to give you many activities you can do to focus on yourself. It will be important for you to do them.

If you really don't want to exercise or if there is some reason why you cannot at this time, you need to find alternate ways to dissipate those chemicals. One of the easiest and most immediate actions you can take when you feel that fight-or flight response kicking in is to focus on your breathing. I like to actually count – I breathe in deeply, counting in my head as I do, "one-two-three" then I breathe out and count again. The counting is sort of a mind trick – if you're focused on counting, you can't be focused on the negative thoughts which caused your response to kick in. As you slow down your breathing in this way, you are signaling to your brain that it is time to relax. This enables your heart rate to slow down, your blood pressure to decrease and those helpful endorphins to be released. Additionally, the relax signal automatically tells your brain to stop sending the cortisol and adrenalin.

Another alternative to exercise is to clean something. For many people, cleaning is a natural response to stress, and with good reason. Cleaning exerts energy and burning that energy helps to release the adrenalin that is being released. It also focuses your mind on an alternative activity and takes your thoughts away from the fear. Trust me, my condo was spotless after my breakup. I even scrubbed my cat!

Food can be another way to manage your stress chemicals. Foods high in tryptophan work to boost your brain's calm mood and relax you. Foods like bananas, oats, soy, milk, cheese, poultry, nuts, peanut butter and sesame seeds are all great resources for tryptophan high foods. At the same time, you should try to avoid the things you're probably craving – foods high in sugar. When your body experiences sugar highs and lows, it responds. The sugar highs will boost you and make you physically more active but when you crash, after the sugar level depletes, your body becomes more susceptible to feelings of fear. You become weary and tired. And, while we're at it, the way around that is not to maintain a high level of sugar in your body. You really do just need to avoid the Ben and Jerry's as much as you can – yes, even the kind with peanut butter in it.

Another great way to relieve stress and relax is to physically cause your body to relax through muscular contraction and relaxation. This requires you to find a place where you can lie down. If you can't find that, at least find a comfortable chair. Sit or lie down and close your eyes. If you can put some relaxing music on your phone or computer while you do this, even better. Next, physically go limp. Feel every single muscle in your body go limp. Take inventory and don't forget areas like fists, your jaw and even your cheeks. Stress causes our bodies to tense up as a protective measure. Forcing your muscles to relax helps to combat this. Once you've gone limp, begin with your toes and tense them up – count to ten then release them. Do your ankles next, then your calves and move up through your body. You may be able to find a guided meditation on YouTube to help you with this process. Go from your toes to the top of your head, tensing and relaxing each area individually.

My last suggestion for you to alleviate stress is to take a hot bath. The heat of the bath water will immediately help your muscles to relax. If you can find some bubble bath that says it helps with stress, even better. Usually eucalyptus/mint combinations will make this claim and will help you relax. Of course, if you're at work, this might not be a possibility but as soon as you get home, jump into the tub. If you dim the lights and light a few candles, you will find the atmosphere even more conducive to relaxation.

Mix in some guided meditation for relaxation and you're well on your way to feeling better.

What is key here is to acknowledge those chemicals when they release and begin to work on countering them as soon as you can. When these chemicals remain in your body for extended periods of time, they can begin to do damage. It is important to release the stress and counter those bad chemicals with good ones as often as you need to.

Science can help you right now, who knew?

Survival Tactic #2

Choose one of the methods above to use right now. If you've only got a few moments or you're reading in public, choose the breathing exercise. Whatever you choose, see it through. Let it work for you. This may mean you sit in a hot tub of water for a while – you may even need to add more hot water. Whatever it takes, do it and feel those stress chemicals leaving your body. Notice that your heart rate slows. Realize that you're not clenching your jaw any more or making fists. Recognize that you no longer feel like you want to run out the door or punch a wall. Let go of the stress you're feeling right now, before reading further.

Chapter 3

How Your Mind Works

I think it's important, before we continue, to get a handle on how your mind works. Most of us are familiar with the terms conscious, subconscious and unconscious mind but how do they play into what we're talking about?

Your Conscious Mind

Most of us think of the conscious mind as being in control. It's the part of your mind you're aware of. It's where you live. The conscious mind is only responsible for about 10% of your brain capacity, though, so while it's the part you're most aware of, it's doing the least work.

If we compare your brain to a computer, the conscious mind is equivalent to the keyboard. You input things through your keyboard and you put things into your brain through your conscious mind (usually). Your conscious mind receives inputs, like criticisms, your self-talk, information you read, this book and millions of other pieces of information and stores it for you.

The conscious mind does not always work on what you're aware of, but on what is going on around you. People who are in a coma or under anesthesia have been shown to have later awareness of things that were said around them or things that happened. This means you can receive inputs and not be aware of them.

We can drill down the two main functions of your conscious mind to these

- Your conscious mind directs your focus

- Your conscious mind has an ability to imagine what is not real

Let's look at how these two functions drive your world and why it is so important for you to make positive changes.

Your conscious mind directs your focus.

Your conscious mind is constantly sending signals to your subconscious mind. You might say the subconscious is obedient to the conscious. If your conscious thoughts are negatively focused, your subconscious mind is sending back negative emotions, thoughts, feelings and memories. It pulls up past events associated with those negative things. It's a protective measure designed to protect you and prepare you for fight or flight in those negative moments. Think of it this way – if someone swings at you and hits you, you may or may not duck the first time, but your subconscious mind stores that information away and the next time someone swings at you, you're more likely to duck. Your mind stored the negative memory of being hit and used that memory to prepare you for being hit again. It's probably a poor example but you get the idea.

The way you need to use this information is to understand that the memories your subconscious is storing can be changed by changing the inputs. Imagine putting wrong data into a computer. The computer won't do what you want it to do because your data is wrong. However, if you realize your mistake and begin inputting the correct data, the computer will do what you want it to do. The same holds for your subconscious. You need to input the correct data, which is positive thoughts, feelings and experiences as well as relaxing and calming thoughts. While it takes time to reprogram your subconscious, you still need to begin at some point for the positive change to occur.

In order to make positive changes in your conscious mind, you must first become aware of what your conscious mind is inputting.

Survival Tactic #3

Even if you don't like to journal, and many don't, I want you to find a notebook and begin keeping track of the thoughts you have regarding yourself. This will take a very dedicated effort but once you start, it will become easier. Listen to your own thoughts. If you trip over your chair at work, what do you say? "You idiot, didn't you see that there?" That is a negative thought because you are calling yourself an idiot. While this seems innocuous, your conscious mind just fed that thought to your subconscious. Your subconscious cannot detect correct from incorrect statements, it simply processes the information, much like the computer attempts to process the incorrect data.

Write down the thoughts you have about yourself, positive and negative and begin to take note of the negatives. When you write down a negative, immediately write a positive. We will continue to develop these positives as this chapter continues. If you want to download a printable worksheet, you can do so here: www.whoholdsthecardsnow.com/hes-gone-now-what-downloads/

Your conscious mind has the ability to imagine what is not real.

Your conscious mind has the ability to visualize things – to imagine. You dream through your consciousness. Your subconscious mind operates only with the memories and data you have fed it previously. It doesn't make up new things. Visualization is a very powerful tool you can use with your conscious mind to alter the data your subconscious mind is processing.

There are many examples of sports teams using visualization to improve their outcomes. In one study, the participants were broken up into three groups. Prior to the study, the group as a whole was given the opportunity to test their accuracy in throwing free throws with a basketball. Following the initial test, the first group was told to practice for 20 days in a row. The second group was told not to practice at all. The third group was told to visualize practicing and, if they missed in their visualization, they were to visualize correcting themselves on the next throw. The results showed that the group who visualized improved by almost as much as the group who practiced every day. The practicing group improved by 24%, the group that did nothing obviously did not improve but the group who visualized practicing improved by 23%.

When you use your conscious mind to visualize positive events in your life, the subconscious mind stores that information away and begins to use that as the new standard. Visualization, like feeding positive thoughts and events, takes time to make a new imprint, but that new imprint can't begin until changes are made.

Survival Tactic #4

Take out a piece of paper and something to write with. Have those in front of you, ready to go. Now, sit somewhere comfortable and close your eyes. Visualize something you want in your life – a new car, a new house, a new boyfriend, a redecorated bathroom, a trip, or anything else that comes to your mind. This is about your dream. Envision everything – what does the leather seating in that new car feel and smell like? Where is your new house? What do the flowers in the garden smell like? What is it like to sit in the tub and relax? Does your new boyfriend have a mustache? How does that feel when you kiss him? Use as many of your senses as you can to envision this dream and really feel the feelings associated. Now, open your eyes and write about what you just envisioned. Write how it felt, the smells, the things you saw. Be as descriptive as you can be about all of those things. Write for as long as it takes to get the whole dream on paper. I've got a worksheet for you to use if you'd like. You can download it here: www.whoholdsthecardsnow.com/hes-gone-now-what-downloads/

The Subconscious Mind

Your subconscious mind is like the memory of your computer. It stores information and calls it up for the functions you perform. Its job is to keep things handy so when you need them, they are quickly retrievable. This means:

- Your memories – how to operate your computer, how to turn on your car or the route you take to work, how much time it takes you to perform a task

- Current programs you're running like how you behave, your habits and your moods

- Your beliefs and values, or the filters you view things through – you use this information to process whether or not something falls within those beliefs and values - you validate things this way

- Each of your senses and the information they provide – sight, hearing, touch, smell and taste

When your subconscious mind cannot process something, it turns to your unconscious for information, which is retrieved and used to make sense of what is happening. Some models indicate that our minds are hit with more than 2 million pieces of information every second. Most of this is processed by your subconscious mind. If your conscious mind processed all of that, you'd be exhausted and overwhelmed within a few minutes of rising in the morning. Instead of your conscious mind processing this information, your subconscious mind takes care of it, filtering it and keeping only what is necessary for your daily functioning. It uses the access it has to your unconscious as a way to decipher what to keep and what to dismiss. Estimates are that of the 2 million pieces of information coming in, maybe 7 are stored for later. That's an amazing ability you have!

What your subconscious does next is to send information back to your conscious mind in the form of emotions, feelings, sensations, reflexes, images and dreams. This communication does not come in the form of words.

The subconscious is obedient.

Your subconscious mind is great in many aspects, but one of the coolest things it does is obey orders. This means that, contrary to what many people think, you are in complete control of what your subconscious is feeding back to your conscious! How? You control the inputs of your conscious mind. If you don't currently think you have control, then you need to make some immediate changes in your thinking! This is scientifically proven stuff!

Survival Tactic # 5

It's time to begin thinking about some reprogramming. This will take a few weeks before it kicks in, but, as the old saying goes, you can't walk a mile until you take the first step. After you've spent some time doing Survival Tactic #3, review the thoughts you've had about yourself. Take any negative thoughts and turn them into positives. This must be done in a specific way, however, so let's look at how.

Negative thought example 1: I am so stupid – I made a huge mistake at work and my boss got mad.

Turn it around: I learn from my mistakes.

This thought, however, is still not positive enough because you have still included a negative word – mistake. Therefore, we must change it further.

Improve the positive: I learn through my experiences.

Now, you've got positive words and positive thoughts. Your turnaround thoughts should never contain the words "can't, don't, won't, not". For example, you should not turn that statement around to simply say "I am not stupid". Your subconscious still hears stupid and doesn't pay attention to the negative "not". If you recall, your subconscious is like the computer memory – it only holds what you tell it and is not able to compute – that's what the computer programs do. Your computer program is your conscious mind so it needs to be the one feeding the positive information to the subconscious in order to have positive results.

Your statement should also be written as if it is current or in the present moment. For example, "I will lose 40 pounds" is not right now – it's a dream you have. You must instead say "I lost 40 pounds". While this is a 'past' statement, you are stating it as if you've already achieved it. "I will stop smoking" isn't good enough. "I am smoke-free" is, but what is even better is "I am healthy because I am smoke-free". This puts the positive of your good health at the forefront of the statement. Your subconscious only sees the here and now, not the future. Keep things in the present and avoid words like "I will be, I am going to, I am getting..." those all point to the future. Also avoid words like "can, would and should". "I can stop smoking" is not nearly as good as "I am healthy because I am smoke-free".

These statements, which we can now officially call affirmations, serve to begin changing the information your subconscious is storing. You are beginning to have full control over the conscious thoughts you are having, which will ultimately have an impact on the information your subconscious feeds back. Over time, no less than a month, you will begin to notice dramatic change. The change will be gradual but in order to see great results, allow yourself a month. This means that, each day, you need to feed these statements to your subconscious.

One final word on these statements before we move on. You don't want to use vague quantitative statements like "more or less". "I want to lose more weight" is not going to get it. "I lost 40 pounds" is much better. Even though you have not yet lost the 40 pounds, it is the information you're feeding to your subconscious that matters, so saying "more" doesn't do any good – more than what? Your subconscious doesn't understand more, less, better, worse, etc. Feed it specifics. "I study more" is not going to get you there but "I study one hour every night" or even better, "I study math for one hour every night". This is present, positive and quantified. Your subconscious can work with this information and begin to store and recall it.

Among your positive statements, you need to have some reaffirming statements like "I am confident", "I am graceful" (great if you're clumsy!), "I am self-reliant" or even things like "I have great legs" or "I have pretty eyes". These statements help you to improve what your subconscious mind spouts back to you and they are important. As before, I have created a worksheet for you to use if you'd like to download it. You can find it here: www.who holdsthecardsnow.com/hes-gone-now-what-downloads/

Your Unconscious Mind

Your unconscious mind is a layer past or deeper than your subconscious. You may recall that we said the subconscious mind will call upon the unconscious mind for memories that are not used as often. Think of your unconscious mind as the library beneath your subconscious. It stores information you input through your conscious mind also, but it's information not used as frequently – not necessary for daily recall. The emotions you've had since birth are stored here. When you want significant and deep, long lasting change, this is the part of your mind you need to access. But how?

It is important to make a distinction between a psychological or psychiatric term unconscious, which is what I have been describing, versus the medical term unconscious, which means under anesthesia or knocked out in some other way. While they have similar qualities, they don't mean the same thing and you shouldn't confuse the two.

We stick things we don't want to remember in our unconscious. Ultra-painful memories are often stored here – abuse is a great example. We stuff them down, so to speak, into our unconscious mind. These memories are not easily triggered and often require psychoanalytical intervention methods like hypnosis to bring them up. These memories can also be triggered by smells or sounds we have associated with the memory. For example, if someone was beaten with a leather strap, the smell of leather may trigger the memory. Smell is a very strong trigger for memories. What is important to remember here is that you cannot recall what is stuffed in the unconscious mind without help or intervention.

What we store in our subconscious can be recalled and that is a main difference between subconscious and unconscious mind. Everything that has happened to you since birth is stored in your unconscious mind. Ultimately, the unconscious and subconscious are storing the same things – thoughts, feelings, memories, habits, emotions and behaviors. The distinction between subconscious and unconscious is that the unconscious is the source file for the subconscious.

In order to change your life at the core in a positive way, you must change the things stored in your unconscious mind. You might be thinking, how? Gregg – how on earth can I change what is stored so deeply? Things since birth? You do it through the direct route – your conscious mind to your subconscious mind, then it shoots off to your unconscious. You input positive thoughts, emotions, behaviors, feelings and habits through the conscious mind. You consciously make changes in those areas. Those changes, especially if visualization is used, get sent to your subconscious mind where they are fed back to you when needed. If this input is often enough and you put all of your energy into it, those memories will begin to overwrite what is stored in your unconscious mind.

Since this is how the negative memories and feelings got to your unconscious in the first place, it only makes sense that you change them through the same method.

Survival Tactic #6

It's time to take things a step further. Back in Tactic 5, you wrote some positive statements. Review them and make sure they pass all of the tests – they are positive, they are written in the present tense, and they are specific. Narrow your list of positive statements, or affirmations, down to maybe 6-10 statements and focus on those first. For the next 30 days, focus on those statements. Write them down on a separate piece of paper and use them throughout your day. If you keep a written calendar, write them at the top of each day. If you have a calendar on your phone or computer. Input them as reminders to trigger throughout your day. What better than to have your phone tell you "You are beautiful inside and out" or "You have great eyes"? It is the repetition that will be your strength at this point. Sure, you may not currently have the confidence you want to have, but if you keep saying "I am a confident woman" to yourself throughout the day, it will start to sink in, literally.

After these sink in, after 30 days of repeating them multiple times a day, add a few from your original list. Do this after you feel that you've nailed the first group and are ready to move on.

I know this chapter was kind of deep and scientific so if it just seemed to be a blur, that's okay. Circle back to it later. It does contain important information for you but if you're not quite ready, no big deal.

Chapter 4

The 9 Stages of Grieving a Relationship

Now that we have a full understanding of how your mind works, it's important to keep that information handy as you begin to proceed through the rest of this book.

Much like you grieve the loss of a loved one in death, you grieve the loss of a relationship. The phases, however are different and they are not at all linear. As you read through these phases, you may see that you've gone in and out of some of them already. You may even revisit some of them. That is normal. Don't think you need to begin with the first one and progress through them to the end. There is also no timeframe in which you should complete each phase. You may stay in one for a day, a week, a month or even a year.

Shock

Shock will almost always be your first phase, based on how it presents. When you go through a breakup, several things happen rather suddenly:

- You find out you're replaceable in the heart of someone you thought would love you forever

- You suddenly feel irrelevant in his life

- You may feel disposable

- You are no longer part of a couple – your identity
  suddenly changed

- All of a sudden, nobody checks up on you at night
  to make sure you got home okay

- All of the familiar sights, sounds, smells, touches
  and even tastes of your life are now different

- Your survival mode kicks in to compensate for the
  foggy, numb, spacey way you feel – your body shifts
  into autopilot

In the shock phase, a new reality kicks in immediately,
forcing you to deal with a lot of altered chemical states
and emotions which can make you feel uncomfortable in
a multitude of ways.

Denial

In the denial phase, you begin to tell yourself the breakup
isn't real. He didn't mean the things he said. This isn't
really happening, not to you. You can't imagine your life
without him in it. You tell yourself he's going through a

stage or a phase and he'll be out of it soon, he'll come to his senses.

Your life continues as if you're still in the relationship. This is part of your primal response to the breakup. Your body is denying the withdrawal process. In order to keep those happy chemicals flowing, your mind is playing tricks and telling you things which, deep inside, you know are not true. You are postponing the grieving process to protect yourself from the pain.

You may not realize you're in denial. This is a subconscious response to the breakup, but, once you do realize you're in the denial phase, you must begin to recognize it as something different – avoidance.

Avoidance, in simplest terms, means you're avoiding facing the truth of the situation. You're avoiding the reality, so you don't have to feel the pain.

Desperate for Answers

In this phase, you go on a full-on search for the 'why' of the breakup. How did this happen to the two of you? Everything was perfect! This phase often comes at the sacrifice of rational thought. You're not thinking logically in this phase.

This search for the why has a purpose. Ultimately, the search for why and how is the first step in disproving those how's and why's. All you have to do is show that the reasons for the breakup are not valid and everything will be okay again.

At some point, you come to the conclusion that there is no good reason for the breakup so you begin to fixate on why those reasons are no good. Your friends may quickly get tired of hanging out with you in this phase because you will tell anybody and everybody how irrational this breakup was. You state and restate all of the reasons you've drummed up in your denial phase.

In all honesty, this phase is sort of a cushion. You're not yet really ready to process the why. You are still in a place where you're avoiding the reality of the loss.

External Bargaining

In this phase, you get creative. If he will take you back, you'll do anything. You will singlehandedly fix everything that was wrong in the relationship. The relationship will be stronger and better than it ever was if he will just let you fix it.

Your ability to use your judgement and reasoning skills is significantly impaired during this phase. You aren't using your full ability to reason that you can't fix it all by yourself. The important question to ask yourself here is whether or not you are the only one at fault for the relationship ending. Would changing everything really solve all of the problems in the relationship?

The truth, which you will discover at some point down the road, is that one person cannot fix all of the wrongs in any relationship. This would be an unreasonable burden to put on yourself, or him, but since you're still in a state of wanting to avoid or alleviate the pain of the breakup, you're not facing what you know to be true – you can't fix it by yourself.

Internal Bargaining

Have you heard yourself start a sentence with this: "If only I had…"?

Uh huh, I thought so. This is the typical sentence starter for the internal bargaining phase. In this phase, you start to internalize all of the problems of the relationship. You envision different outcomes to all of the problems of the relationship.

- If only I had picked him up at the airport instead of making him take a cab

- If only I had kept up with the laundry

- If only I hadn't pushed him into buying that bigger house

The reality of the situation is that those things didn't happen that way and you can't go back in time, unless you've invented a time machine, to fix things. Much as we'd all like to, we can't change the past. The second half of this phase is that you can't guarantee that picking him up at the airport or doing the laundry in a timelier manner would have changed anything.

Relapse

It is possible that this breakup isn't the first for the two of you. You may have broken up and gotten back together once or twice before. This only feeds into this phase, which is the phase where you manage to convince him to reconcile with you or at least you give it the old college try!

This is yet another effort to alleviate the pain of the split and restart the flow of those happy chemicals your body craves. The problem is that the hurts from the past are still there and they will rear their ugly heads sooner or later. Getting back together, especially if you've begged your way back in, is temporary at best. Neither of you has changed, nor have you likely given any real discussion to the problems of the relationship before the split.

You are not only avoiding the pain of the split, but you're avoiding the possibility of life after the split. You don't want to think about what your life might look like without him in it. That's too difficult to imagine at this point.

This is yet another phase where you are delaying the pain of the breakup.

Initial Acceptance

Finally, right? You're beginning to accept the breakup. You have moments of clarity where you can see yourself living your life without him but those moments of clarity are often mixed in with irrational moments filled with elements of the other phases.

You will go in and out of initial acceptance a few times, especially early on. As you progress, if you set yourself on a healthy healing course, your time in this phase will get longer and longer. In this phase, you begin to resist contacting him when you're accepting of the break. Of course, in your relapse moments, you will fall down again and probably reach out.

Over time, your successes in accepting the breakup will grow stronger and last longer. You will begin to put boundaries in place which align with your values and help you begin to see your life in the future instead of dwelling on the past.

Your first few times in the initial acceptance phase will be quick and you won't feel like you've gotten anywhere, but each time you come into this phase, you will find more success. It will build and build until you are able to get through it to another phase.

Anger

Anger takes many forms, depending on how soon after the breakup you're feeling it. In the beginning, you will turn this anger on yourself. You will look to your own shortcomings and blame yourself for what happened. You get angry with yourself for causing the breakup. Some really nice negative self-talk can come in here. Stuff like:

- I'm too fat

- I'm too ugly

- I'm too stupid

In the anger phase, your main goal is to place blame. Venting anger is one way to do that. You'll know you've finally gotten over the anger phase when you realize you're angry over the breakup and no longer are trying to place blame.

The trick is to learn how to be responsible for your own anger. When you reach a point where you can do that, you will find that you are able to pull together the pieces of your life and begin to move forward. This anger (the anger over the breakup) gives you the energy to move forward.

Hope

Hope takes many forms during the process of grieving a relationship. In the early phase, hope takes the form of hoping you will get back together. The result for you is to do anything and everything to revive the relationship.

Hopelessness is one of the worst emotions we can feel as humans. It is a truly desperate emotion. The only time human beings truly lose hope is when they are facing death. This means that, even in your worst feeling of hopelessness for the relationship, you can still access some sense of feeling hopeful instead.

As your grief progresses, your hope will shift from hoping the relationship can be saved to hoping you will survive without it. This shows a definite positive progression as you are beginning to see your life without him in it.

As you get to that point, you begin to build on your accomplishments. Each small thing you accomplish – each goal you reach or small victory you have in some area, will build into bigger and bigger accomplishments and victories.

What Does It Mean?

I have no doubt you can see yourself in several of these phases already. It is possible to be in more than one at a time and, as I said in the beginning, it is possible to come into and go out of these phases numerous times.

Don't beat yourself up if you get stuck in one phase or another for a while. Don't let your friends tell you that you need to move through these phases faster or that what you're feeling is silly or unnecessary. Each of these phases is necessary to move you through to a healthier, more confident woman.

What Can You Do?

It is important for you to recognize that what you are experiencing is normal. Regardless of which phase you can most identify with right now, it's normal. Short of the shock phase, you won't go through these phases in the order they're presented here. You may skip some. You may stay in some phases for what seems to your friends and family to be 'too long'. Kindly tell them that you need to process this in your own time, not theirs and keep plugging along.

Having said that, it is important for you to be doing the work throughout this book, regardless of which phase you're in. Some of the work has obvious benefits to specific phases and some of the work hasn't even been presented to you yet. Where you are sucks. I know that. I also know that you might not feel like doing the work today. It may just feel too overwhelming. I get it. I'm not here to push you through a process you're not ready to go through. What I am here for is to be your coach, your guide. I am here to present to you the tools I know will help you.

I promise that you will feel better after you do the work I'm giving you in this book. The sooner you get after it, the better.

As your coach, I'm going to tell you not to wallow in self-pity, at least for very long. The whole 'woe is me' thing is not going to get you anywhere. Feel it for a little while – allow yourself some specific amount of time, but never more than a few days at the most. Then, it's time to pick yourself up, dust yourself off and go find something to shift your energy and focus. I know there are days you may not even feel like getting out of bed but those are the days that we're trying to get rid of with this book and the activities I give you. If you don't feel like you can get out of bed, close your eyes and visualize yourself doing something fun like having lunch with a good friend or going out to buy a new pair of shoes. New shoes fix everything for women from what I understand. Visualize a vacation you want to take or that new car you've been wanting to buy. Soon, the positive vibes from the visualization will motivate you out of your funk.

Survival Tactic #7

Identify the phase you are in today. Right now, which one or which ones do you best identify with? Remember, you can be experiencing things from more than one phase at a time. Now that you can identify with a phase, use the information in this chapter to understand what you're feeling and use some of the tactics I have given you so far to work through it.

For example, if you're in the Desperate for Answers phase, you need to read the next chapter where we talk about closure. If you're in the External Bargaining phase, you need to recognize that one person cannot affect change on a relationship. You read it in the words above but now, really begin to take them to heart. We are going to spend a little time working through some of the issues of these phases in the upcoming chapters. For now, recognize your phase and start to realize the miscues your subconscious is sending you. Write down the negative thoughts and write some affirming thoughts to counter them.

You may not see the point in doing some of these Survival Tactics as you're doing them, but trust the process. I wouldn't needlessly give you things to do. I know how valuable your time is! These Survival Tactics are worth your precious time!

PHASE 2
Getting Past the Breakup

Now that you have a full understanding of what you're feeling and why, it's time to begin the hard work of getting past the breakup. I know, your life still sucks and you're no happier than you were when you started reading. Remember, though, you didn't get here in one day and you won't dig your way out in one day either. Your relationship lasted a while. The memories you made together happened over time. It will take time to reprogram those memories. As you read, it will take time to change the things you're storing in your unconscious and subconscious.

Chapter 5

Why You Must Go
No Contact
and How

WARNING: Using no contact with a man can cause him to want to pursue again. It's the nature of how the male mind works. Be aware that when you go no contact with your ex, he may pursue you, even if he was the one to break up to begin with. Prepare for this and strengthen your resolve. Continue to go no contact, even if he attempts to contact you. You're doing this so you can heal. It is not meant to be a game you play with your ex.

Do you know what bothers me the most about break-ups? They rarely end quickly like they should. Breakups drag on unmercifully like a wound that will never heal. They persist for weeks, months and even years as the couple tries again and again thinking, "This time it will be different."

It won't be. At least not right now. In order to have a different outcome, one or both of you must make a change for the better. Let's not kid ourselves here, you are breaking up because this relationship needs to be over. Reconciliation is not an option, at least not now, so it's time to stop trying to formulate a plan to get him back. That isn't why you're reading this book. You're reading to get over him – to move past the breakup in a healthy way, not to get back with him.

Relationships need to end suddenly. The door to reopen that relationship needs to be closed for good. You need to unfriend him on social media and block him. Not only do you not need to see what he's up to but he doesn't need to see what you're up to. I know you will be hesitant to do this but it is necessary. This won't be easy, and you will fight me on it but your mind is not working in a logical way right now so I'm going to ask you to trust me.

A breakup is not a linear process. It is complicated. Kids are just one way in which you and your ex may always need to have some level of contact. It's like some cruel joke as you try to recover in vain. When there are children in the picture or you have a financial connection like a home, or some other connection not easily broken (you work together, etc.), you will need to have contact. We are going to address how to manage these situations shortly.

What we want to do here is smooth the bumps a little bit so the ride is less harsh. I have one goal and that is your recovery from the extreme pain and sense of loss you're feeling. Remember what we learned early in the book. Breaking the addiction to this relationship will be at least as difficult, if not more so, as breaking an addiction to crack cocaine.

Your contact with your ex is like the drug delivery system – your crack pipe if you will. If you're trying to break a crack habit, what do you do with the pipe? You break your connection to it – you get rid of it. Your communication with your ex is your crack pipe so it must go. You don't try to stop drinking alcohol by keeping a bottle of gin around. You don't stop smoking by keeping a pack of cigarettes on your desk. It's all the same.

You have the why, now let's talk about how

Hopefully, you now understand that no contact is a key tool in breaking your addiction to your relationship. Let's look at how you go about it.

When Kids Are Involved

If you and your ex have children together, you will need to maintain some level of contact. This means you will always have to see him. You will always need to communicate about the children. That's your key – your communication now needs to be only about the children. Depending on what type of person your ex is and who initiated the breakup, he may try to take advantage of these times to pick a fight or beg you to come back.

You need to strengthen your resolve before you enter these situations. You need to be able to say, without a quiver in your voice and without hesitation, "Let's keep our conversation strictly about the kids."

Use a rule of 3 with your ex. What this means is you allow someone to repeat their request no more than three times. If he continues, you simply shut him down. It's possible you were in a relationship where he felt as if he could control you. You standing up to him is not only important to your growth but it's important to you improving your level of self-confidence. To use the rule of three, you repeat the same thing the first two times but if and when the third instance comes up, you shut it down. Let's look at an example:

Steve: "Jen, I don't understand why you felt the need to end our relationship"

Jen: "Steve, let's keep our conversation to the kids. Sammy needs his antibiotic three times a day and Steph needs to finish her math homework this weekend."

Steve: "Okay but why can't we talk about this?"

Jen: "Steve, let's keep our conversation to the kids."

Steve: "Jen, please, tell me why we can't try to work this out."

Jen: "I'll meet you at 4 on Sunday to get the kids."

At this point, Jen turns and walks away. She either goes back in the house or gets into her car, depending on where they are. Of course, she would say any goodbyes to the kids, etc. but her conversation with Steve is over.

This is important for two reasons. She is sending Steve two signals. The first is that she isn't willing to discuss or argue over their past relationship. Two is she is setting boundaries and we will go into that more later.

When You Work Together

A workplace romance is never a good idea, so let's begin there. Sometimes, however, it is unavoidable. In those circumstances, you're left with a lot of gossip behind your back, the possibility of daily contact and the continuous reminder of your ex, whether you want it or not.

The first thing you need to do is not discuss your relationship or your breakup with anyone at work. Even if you and your best friend work together as well, the workplace is not where you talk about relationship issues. In addition to that, you and your ex need to avoid any relationship discussion – at all but especially at work. The same tactics apply as those I outlined for communicating about the kids – the rule of three.

The only difference is that, in a workplace environment, you need to maintain a higher level of civility. In order to keep from losing your cool, you need to be mentally prepared to have a difficult, but brief conversation. Let's look at how that might go.

Jon: "Amber, can we get together and talk?"

Amber: "No, Jon."

Jon: "Amber, I'd really like to talk about us."

Amber: "No, Jon,"

Jon: "Amber, please let's meet after work for drinks. For old time's sake?"

Amber: "I'm sorry Jon, I've got a phone call I need to make."

Amber has applied the rule of three. She gave Jon the opportunity to listen to what she said – and she said "No." She didn't supply, nor did she need to supply an excuse or any reasoning and you shouldn't either. The more you talk, the more openings you give someone to argue with your no. No is no.

You Share Property Or Assets

This is probably the easiest communication to drop. If need be, you can hire an attorney to be your proxy for any final dispersion of assets, sale of property, etc. If, however, you don't want to or cannot afford to hire an attorney to stand in for you, then the same rule – the rule of three – applies. Let's look at how this works.

Brian: "The closing for our house is next Friday. Do you want to get together after and talk?"

Kayla: "No. What time is the closing?"

Brian: "4:00 – perfect timing to grab dinner at our favorite place after."

Kayla: "Brian, I can't."

Brian: "Come on Kayla, I know you love to go there. Just friends I promise!"

Kayla: "I need to go now. Thank you for the information. I'll see you at the closing."

Regardless of how hard he tries or what language he uses, your answer needs to remain the same. "No." Keep your communication focused on the topic at hand – the closing of your home. Avoid any and all attempts he may make to extend the meeting to before or after.

You never owe an explanation. Period.

We often feel we need to explain our responses. "I'm sorry Brian, I don't want to have dinner with you on Friday" does not leave him thinking you really said "No". It means "Maybe another time" or "Not now". This is why you must use as few words as possible. Resist the urge to explain why. Why is irrelevant.

Let's Clarify What No Contact Means

So we are on the same page and you don't cheat on the process, let's define exactly what no contact means, assuming you are not required to talk for the three reasons mentioned above.

No texts, emails or phone calls

This one makes sense and it is the easiest to understand. Do not call, do not text, do not email your ex. If you have things that belong to him, think about contacting a mutual friend to intervene and deliver his things. You can also send them to him but do not put any type of note in the box or envelope. Just send his things.

No drive-bys

No contact also means you don't drive by his house, his office, his gym or his favorite Friday night hang out. You and I both know this is a way to stay connected. Is his car there? Who is he with? Is he as broken up as you are?

Don't do it. When the urge to get in your car and go find him creeps up, call a girlfriend or get a book to read. Do anything else except cave in to that urge.

No social media

Block, unfriend or unfollow him on social media. Delete him from your Snapchat and any other forms of communication you may have. We talked about this in the beginning of the chapter. This seems to be the hardest part for women to commit to but it is extremely important. You do not need to know what he's up to right now and he doesn't need to know what you're doing either. Social media is for friends and right now, we can't consider the two of you to be friends. Some time down the road, maybe you will be friends but your grief and pain cannot manage that connection right now so be strong and do as I tell you.

No hookups

Don't think for one minute that you can just have sex with your ex and then walk away without feeling anything. While it's tempting to hook up with your ex, don't do it. I don't care how great the sex was, it's only going to serve to set you back in your recovery. While it might seem like a good thing, it won't be. I know a man who did the whole, one time for old time's sake hookup with his ex and she ended up pregnant. They tried to get back together, but of course, it didn't work and instead, they brought a little boy into a world where his parents were already divorced. Did I mention they were both in their early 40's? This can happen to you. Don't do it.*

Chapter 6

Your Need for Closure

No doubt, you have expressed, at least to yourself, if not to your friends and family, a need for closure. Let's examine closure and whether or not you really need to have it.

Closure can be best defined as the need to have answers to a question. When someone is murdered, the family always feels as if bringing the murderer to justice will provide closure. They will know the why, but the truth is that knowing the why doesn't change the outcome for them and it won't change the outcome for you.

You want to formulate an answer to something which feels unanswered – the reason seems ambiguous to you and this causes you to feel a multitude of emotions – anxiety, fear, pain. The reason many seek closure is either that they want to feel they have the ability to predict the future or they want a stronger basis to take action in some way. I can predict your future right now. If you do the work to heal in a healthy way from this breakup, your future and your ability to find a great man who won't leave is great. If you avoid doing the work you need to do, you're destined to repeat past relationship mistakes. We're going to work on this soon.

Often, people may feel they need closure immediately – this is called urgency. They may also feel that they want to maintain a feeling of closure for as long as possible – this is the permanency tendency. When you combine these two tendencies, you may do what is often called "seizing and freezing". This means your ability to process information properly is impaired and you may miss obvious judgement cues. Your thinking is biased.

At the end of a relationship, closure means knowing why your relationship ended and not feeling that you have an emotional attachment to that person again – or in your illogical thought process, getting him back. Your true goal is not to feel any more pain or anxiety over the situation and you feel closure will give that to you.

Why is this need for closure so important to us? Because we like to think in stories. We make sense of things in terms of stories. Good attorneys will give the jury a story, whether it's the story the prosecution wants to tell to make the jury believe their perpetrator did the crime or it's the defense telling the jury an alternative story of what could have happened – a story which does not include their client. We create stories in our head to fit our own narratives. Our stories have a beginning, a middle and an end.

I know a woman who creates stories, which are completely fictional, when someone she loves hurts her in some way. When her sister didn't answer her phone call on the sister's birthday, this woman created a story, over the span of a few days, about how her sister must be angry with her and she also fabricated the why. Of course, none of this is true but meanwhile, she is prepared to write a letter to her sister, itemizing the reason she's sure her sister is angry with her and addressing this. The problem with this whole story is that she made the whole thing up, and she is about to unnecessarily create a tenuous situation between herself and her sister if she sends her letter. Sometimes, our stories have no basis of fact. This is dangerous.

When your ex left, or when you ended the relationship, you lost the original story. In the original story, there was a happy beginning, middle and end. Unfortunately, when he left, you needed to change the story. Your ending changed. The new story needs to fit what you're perceiving of the situation at that time. If he left, your initial story may be that he found someone else or he got scared by commitment or maybe he just got tired of being tied down. If you initiated the breakup, you created your story before you left. Whether or not your story about the break up is true is irrelevant. It's what is giving you peace at this time.

In your original story, the one with the happy ending, you both lived happily ever after, until death do us part. When the relationship ended, your happy story was disrupted – what was once safe – your relationship – is now more like a vacuum that feels like it's sucking the life out of you. It's an abyss. Seeking closure helps you to rewrite the story in a different, perhaps healthier way. Without that closure, you may feel as if you have tons of questions. You may question who you are and what you're all about now. Depending on how long you were together, you may feel as if you've completely lost your identity. You were part of a couple but now, you're not.

The problem with seeking closure is that, in the end, it may or may not give you the answers you're looking for. There are only certain answers which will really satisfy you and the odds of you getting the answers you want are not all that great.

Another problem is that your ex may or may not be interested in answering your questions. Chances are, he won't be. If he left, he may have already moved on. If you left him, he may feel bitter and angry. Instead of looking to your ex for closure, I have some things you can do to get closure in a way that will lead you to healing.

Survival Tactic #8

Instead of seeking closure from your past relationship, write the story of your next six months. Today is your beginning so write about where you are right now, then write the middle, and finish up with a happy ending. You can write about whatever you want. Write about the healing process or about the new things you're going to try or about what you want to do in your career. Your story contains everything in your life, not just your relationship so include things other than your relationship. Think of this as a first swipe at what you want to accomplish in the next 6 months. We know 6 months from now isn't the end of your story, but let's just make it about that length of time for now. When you write, think about your past as well.

Note If you've read any of my other books or been on my website, you may have seen me talk about your story. That's not what I am referring to here. In that instance, your story is more about your past experiences and what types of things you're good at or interested in. Write this story or narrative about your next 6 months.

Chapter 7

It's Time to
Take Care of You

Women are especially bad at taking care of themselves. As natural nurturers, they take care of others at the expense of taking care of their own well-being, both physical and mental. Those days are over. And don't tell me you don't have time. If you have kids, your ex should have them for at least an evening or two once a week or so. You can't afford not to take the time to take care of yourself.

This is a great time to start reading the book I gave you, *Own Your Tomorrow*. If you haven't emailed me yet for your free copy, you can now by emailing me at Gregg@ WhoHoldsTheCardsNow.com. Don't forget to put **ICAN** in the subject line. I will email the free book to you as soon as I can. Please give me a day to do so.

Why?

In order to be a good partner in a relationship, you need to learn how to become an individual. Step one in this is to recognize that you deserve a little of your own attention. In order to give yourself this attention, you need to spend some time alone.

Don't turn the page...I see the fear forming in your eyes. Yes, I said you need to spend some time alone. It is imperative that you get comfortable being by yourself and there are several very valid reasons.

You learn who you are.

In your alone time, you have the chance to really get in your own head and dig out who you really are. In the last phase of this book we're going to really dig into this a little more. You'll be defining your ideal self and uncovering your values, as a single woman.

You need to do some self-assessment, work through the survival tactics in this book and really get to know yourself again. When we get into relationships, we sacrifice pieces of who we are. Our partner doesn't like sports so we drift away from them over time. Our partner loves antique cars so we learn more about them but never really get whole-heartedly into them. We lose sight of ourselves.

Now that you're single, it's the perfect time to find out what it is you do like. I've had coaching clients dig into becoming a writer, learning a new sport, skydiving, adult coloring books and a host of other hobbies and activities they never would have pursued if they were still with their ex. This is your time to truly find what you enjoy. Embrace it!

You become independent.

I hear your argument. You're already independent. No. Chances are you are not independent. Independent women in relationships do not give up their needs, wants or desires for the man in their life or for the good of the relationship. Women do this more often than men. As soon as a woman finds a man, she will stop doing things she once did in lieu of spending time with her man. While a man may act as if he wants all of this time from a woman, he really doesn't and he will soon begin to pull back.

Independent women also tend to believe that they can't be happy doing things if they aren't doing them with their boyfriend, so they gauge their participation on him. If the boyfriend doesn't want to see a movie, regardless of how badly the girlfriend wants to see it, she won't. If she wants to go on a weekend getaway to the mountains with friends and he doesn't, she won't go. You end up miserable but still feeling as if you're in love. You had a false sense of what it means to be happy and you gave up pieces of yourself for your boyfriend. Trust me when I say that no man wants you by his side 24/7. No man wants to do everything with his girlfriend.

Independent women also see when a relationship has gone bad and they get out before more damage is done. They recognize that things have gotten toxic and they end it. A dependent woman will stay in the relationship out of fear that there isn't anyone else who wants her anyway so what the heck. An independent woman knows that there are other fish in the sea and if there aren't, she's comfortable being alone because it's better than giving herself up for a man who doesn't value her.

Independent women also don't feel the need to control others. This type of woman isn't constantly checking up on her boyfriend to see if he's where he said he was going to be or if he's doing what he said he was going to do. When he's out doing his thing, she's out with her friends doing her thing or she's enjoying a peaceful night at home, alone with a good book and a glass of wine.

Independent woman also hold themselves and those around them to high standards. They have values and they know what they will and will not accept out of the people they interact with. Independent women have no problem setting boundaries (coming up later) and holding people to them.

Hopefully, you're beginning to see why becoming independent is so important. I'll show you how soon!

You get out of your head and his.

Right now, you may still be focused on wondering why your breakup happened or how it happened. You may spend hours rehashing different conversations or situations, wishing you could do things differently. You can't, and furthermore, even if you did, you can't guarantee the outcome would be any different. When you recognize you're in this phase, you need to repeat this short phrase to yourself – "It doesn't matter". The why and how no longer matter. It just is.

What matters is the here and now, and your future. You cannot look forward and backward at the same time. You need to choose.

How?

Stop worrying.

If you are worrying about something, you need to ask yourself one simple question: can you do anything to help or change the situation? If the answer is no, you may as well stop worrying about it right now because you cannot affect change. If the answer is yes, then get on with doing whatever it is you need to do. If the answer is you don't know, then find out.

Worrying is our way of anticipating an unknown future. We imagine outcomes that may or may not happen. It is anxiety in high gear. The truth is we cannot predict the future. We don't know what will happen 5 minutes from now and for some, that unknown is extremely uncomfortable, so they fret over it.

Rather than fretting over something that hasn't happened or something you don't control, try living in the here and now. You're missing out on a lot of good stuff happening around you while you worry about things that may never even happen.

Be grateful.

If I catch myself living too much in my head, I stop and think about everything I have to be grateful for. The easiest way to be grateful is to take time, every evening or morning to write out some gratitude statements. Shoot for 5 unique statements every day for a month. Yes, you might catch yourself being grateful for flexible garbage bags but who cares? The point of this exercise is to help you see all of the wonderful in your life. When you begin to see all of the good things in your life, it becomes more difficult to focus on the negatives.

Focus on your surroundings.

We are, by nature, very self-conscious. This causes us to be very anxious. Some people won't sing in their cars when they're driving by themselves because of what other drivers might think. Hey, if those other drivers aren't watching the road, you'd better be more worried about them crashing into you than judging you for singing.

Dancing is another activity many feel uncomfortable with and for the same reason. Instead of focusing on what you're thinking, focus on how your body is interacting with your surroundings. If you're sitting in a comfy chair, focus on allowing your body to really relax into the chair. Really sink into it, close your eyes and just enjoy the comfort of that chair.

Be aware of the beauty around you. I love taking walks in nature, even in the winter. I enjoy the solitude and the quiet. I enjoy listening to figure out what animals I might hear or if I hear birds chirping. I like hearing the leaves or snow crunch under my feet. I like seeing the sun shine through the leaves or down onto the snow. Observe and be amazed by what is around. If you're not doing this, you're truly missing out.

Allow yourself to lose track of time.

This can be challenging for women because many times in your life, you need to be picking someone up or dropping someone off for some lesson or another. Take some time when you're by yourself and just let go of time. If you really have an appointment or something you have to do at a set time, set an alarm or timer. Then, get out a good book, light some candles and put on some relaxing music or just sit with your eyes closed and let time pass without worrying about what's next. It's okay to do this. Tell yourself that.

Face your pain head on — don't run.

Our inclination, when we face fear or pain, is to run from it – to try to avoid it. People do this in a variety of ways. Some bury themselves deep into something, almost to a point of obsession. Others turn to drugs or alcohol. Still others just bury the pain to avoid feeling it. This is your mind working to protect you.

The problem is that we begin to have emotions about our emotions. They go a level deeper. For example, when your breakup was fresh, you felt sad, heartbroken and you may long for him. If you don't acknowledge the pain, it compounds. You might say something like "I hate this" or "I hate feeling like this". You might think you need to make the feelings go away. You become sad about feeling sad. The problem is that in saying these things, you're actually prolonging your sadness and heartbreak. You're focusing on it, but not in a way that will allow it to pass.

What you need to do instead is to tell yourself it's okay to feel how you feel. Don't wish the feelings away without feeling them first. Rather than "I hate feeling like this", you should tell yourself, "It's okay to feel this way right now. This will get better." Read and reread the first Phase of this book. Everything you're feeling is normal.

Saying this doesn't mean you like where you are. It simply means you acknowledge it. You're not stuffing the pain or avoiding it. You're allowing yourself to feel it and you're telling yourself it's okay to feel it and that it will go away.

Engage in your environment.

Have you ever been reading a book and you realize that while you read the words, you can't remember what they were? Maybe you were driving and lost track of 15 minutes. I make a long drive to my sister's bed and breakfast and occasionally, I'll find myself completely zoned out and for a minute or two, I'm not sure where in my drive I am. I'm in an area where everything kind of looks the same so it takes me a few minutes to get my bearings.

To avoid having this happen, be aware of your surroundings. Find new things to observe. We zone out because everything is so familiar. I zone out on my drive because I've seen all of the sights before. To avoid this, I look for things I haven't seen before. Are the leaves turning color? Are there flowers blooming somewhere? I become engaged in my surroundings. In this way, I'm staying present in the moment. I am in the here and now, rather than zoning out. I recognize that change is always occurring around me.

Survival Tactic #9

Begin a gratitude journal or list. Grab some sort of notebook and start writing 5 new things you are grateful for every day. Do this for a month. Each new item should be different than those before. It sounds like it will be hard and yes, you might be grateful for your cup of coffee or 5 more minutes of sleep but the point is to begin to appreciate the good in your life. If that 5 minutes of sleep was good, be grateful for it! I've prepared a gratitude page for you if you'd like to download it. You can find it at http://www. whoholdsthecardsnow.com/hes-gone-now-what-downloads.

Chapter 8

End the Obsessing

No doubt, you've found yourself obsessing about your ex and the breakup. It's a natural part of the process you're going through. It may seem difficult to move past these thoughts but this chapter is about providing you with the tools you need to do just that.

You may be shaking your head right now, "No way, Gregg, I'm not obsessing". Okay, well let's just look at a little checklist. If you pass, great! But, don't skip this chapter because even if you're not obsessing, you still need to take the steps in this chapter.

Without further ado, you're obsessing if:

- You find any excuse to contact him (remember our no contact rule)

- You find it difficult to resist the urge to call or text him – you probably even break the no contact rule

- You drive by or park outside of his workplace

- You drive by his house or apartment at night

- You check in with his best friends, stalk them on social media or just happen to show up where you know they all hang out, hoping to find out what he's up to

- Your thoughts and actions are more about him and less about you

How Do You Stop?

The best way to stop thinking so much about him is to focus your thoughts elsewhere.

"Gee, Gregg, I never thought of that" (insert sarcasm).

I know, I know but hang in there with me. Right now, you're in this place where you sometimes feel an overwhelming need to know he's at least as miserable as you, if not more. He wouldn't dare be out having fun already and you want to make sure. You want him to be suffering like you are so you need to check.

Instead, when you feel him creeping into your thoughts, you need to find something else to focus your thoughts on. Not only is this good for diverting your thoughts from your ex, but it's good for writing your story. In

Phase 3, we will get into this more. For now, what you need to know is that your story is what makes you interesting. You already have a story, which is great, but you also need to continue to write the story of you. The same pathway to writing the story of you is the one that you walk to end the obsessing. (This is not the same story you wrote earlier) Nice right?

Get rid of relationship reminders.

I knew a man once who kept every gift his ex-wives and ex-girlfriends had given him. This was very difficult for new women in his life. I don't have to tell you women don't like reminders of the women from the past.

Look around and get rid of things he bought you. If one of those things is an engagement ring, you should return it. Otherwise, donate the things he gave you. Someone else won't know the history of the item and they will enjoy having it.

Find a hobby.

Hobbies can best be described as something you do to occupy your hands and mind. For men, this might be refurbishing old cars, woodworking, photography, cooking, yardwork or many other hobbies. For you, it might be one of those, or it might be sewing, scrapbooking, art, knitting, or whatever it is you're interested in. Think of a hobby as something you do when you want to pull your

thoughts away from obsessive thoughts. It's something
you can, and should, get lost in for a while.

If you don't have a hobby now, try a few things you've
always wanted to do. An easy way to do this is to either
join a Meetup group (MeetUp.com) or to go to a local
store which offers supplies for what you want to do.
Often, they offer classes. Take a class and see if you like it.

Get passionate about something.

I love animals, especially cats. I like to take care of them,
I like to volunteer at shelters. I like owning them. What
is your passion? Is it art or animals? Maybe it's politics or
some other cause. Whatever it is, find a group that shares
your passion and join in. Get involved with people who
share your passion. (psst…this is a great way to meet men
with your same interest!)

Phone a friend.

Get your mind off of your thoughts by meeting up with
a friend or close family member. If you can't shift your
thoughts away from him, call someone and go do something. The best way to divert your thoughts is to change
activities. Don't sit there and dwell on him.

Get busy.

The suggestions I've given you have all centered around
getting busy. Get your calendar out and fill it with activities. Fill it with hobbies, passions, friends and family. Fill

it with trips you've wanted to take or local places you've always wanted to see. Do the things you didn't do but didn't because your boyfriend or husband didn't want to.

The point of getting busy is two-fold. First, it helps you get your mind off of things. Second, it helps you write your story. An added bonus is that when you do get into dating again, having a full calendar insulates you from diving head-first into a relationship before it's time. Men love to pursue a woman, it keeps their interest in you piqued. We'll talk more about this in Phase 3 but for now, know that it's going to be okay to say, "I'm sorry Rob, I can't go out on Friday but I'm free Sunday." Busy!

What else?

You may have other ideas of how to distract yourself. If you enjoy some activity like hiking, horseback riding or skiing, go for it. The idea is to take yourself out of that moment of obsessing and redirect your thoughts.

Another thing you should be doing throughout each day is repeating your affirmations. When you are obsessing is a great time to redirect to affirmations. It takes the focus off of your ex and puts it where it should be right now, on you.

What I've given you here are just some ideas. I strongly urge you to find a new hobby because it is good for your overall mental health and having things you're passionate about makes you interesting to others but my point is this – do something different and redirect your thoughts. Each time you do it, it will become easier and, before you know it, those obsessive thoughts will be all but gone.

Survival Tactic #10

Go to Meetup.com or a hobby or craft store and investigate a hobby. Find something you can begin to enjoy. Sign up for a class or look online on YouTube or some other site for instructions. Learn something about your new hobby. If you don't like it, choose another. That's an okay thing to do.

Survival Tactic #11

What are you passionate about? What really gets your emotions stirred up? Special Olympics? Animal Welfare? Politics? Homeless? Find something and begin looking into opportunities to get involved. You don't actually have to go do something yet, unless you're ready. I want you to have an arsenal of tools available to you when you are ready to get back out into the world and begin to bury yourself in activities.

Chapter 9

Taking Inventory on Relationships

We are now going to begin doing the real recovery work! Exciting, right? You've read a lot about how your mind and body have been impacted by this breakup. Soon, we're going to learn about happiness and values but first, we need to take inventory.

While this is presented at this point in the book, it isn't necessary for you to complete the two inventories in this chapter and the next before reading on. In fact, don't. I don't want you to rush through them, but I do want you to proceed through your healing process. Completing these inventories can take a while, depending on where you are in the grieving and healing process. If you're feeling pretty strong at this point, you may spend a few evenings working on them and feel pretty good but chances are, you will go through these at a slower pace, as you should. As with the rest of the process, don't let anyone tell you you're going to slow or too fast. Go at your own pace.

The Relationship Inventory

Chances are, you're not viewing your relationship through logical, realistic lenses right now. You may be blaming yourself more than necessary, or him more than necessary. You're looking at things in a very one-sided way. That is to be expected but in order to heal and press on, a more realistic look at the relationship is required.

When you remember certain parts of the relationship but block out others, it's called splitting and it is an unhealthy way to look at the relationship. When you're splitting, you're looking at things in an unrealistic and highly emotional way. This is normal for what you're going through but that doesn't mean we can't make a course correction! In order for you to truly move past this relationship, you need to look at it for what it really was, not for what you're choosing to remember, whether good or bad.

Before you begin, there are a few 'rules'. First of all and most importantly, do not push yourself past what is emotionally comfortable. What I mean by this is that if doing one of the steps causes you to cry, cry it out. Walk away from it for a while and regain perspective. If you get angry or frustrated, same rule applies. Walk away. You can't be really honest and do this inventory correctly if your emotions are that high.

If you would like to download my relationship inventory worksheet, you can do so here. If you prefer to just get a paper and pencil, go for it. You don't need to do these steps in order. In fact, you probably will jump back and forth between them as things come to you. Read them all over first and then go back and fill in what comes to mind. Allow yourself as much as a week or two to complete these. You won't think of everything at once, things will come to you over time. Once you've completed all of the questions, give yourself a break, pat yourself on the back and recognize how difficult this was. For a few days, don't do any work on this inventory and don't proceed with the next just yet. Take a break from it all and do some things for yourself. Get out Own Your Tomorrow and do some of the activities in there or work on one of your new hobbies or passions.

1. The Relationship Positives

This might be a real challenge but this is important. Think back to the good things about the relationship. What things did you do together that you enjoyed? Were there friends you enjoyed hanging out with? Were there family events or vacations where you had a great time? You're in one place or the other right now – you either only remember the good times or the bad. Either way, be realistic about what was good and what you truly enjoyed.

2. The Positive Qualities of Your Ex

You're either missing him terribly right now and all you see are his good qualities or you really want to punch his lights out and you can't see any positive qualities. Either way, write down what was good about him. Is he generous? Did he randomly send you flowers or was he always willing to help others? Find his good qualities and make a list.

3. Special Things

Make a list of either 5 special things your ex did for you or 5 special times during your relationship. This one can be tricky, again, depending on where you are in your like or dislike of your ex right now but there were things that fit into one or both of these categories.

4. Friends and Family

What did your friends and family like about him? Don't say nothing – surely there was something they liked? If you're not sure, ask them. If they ask why you want to know, tell them you are trying to move forward from the breakup and this will help.

5. What did You like that They Didn't?

Usually, friends and family are pretty quick to point out things about your partners that you don't see. We put on those rose-colored glasses in relationships and begin to become blind to the faults of our partners. After you make a list of what they didn't like that you did, write about who was right. Did they see things you truly were blind to or do you think they just misunderstood him? When they raised concerns or objections, did you defend him or try to excuse his behavior?

6. Relationship Negatives

What was negative in the relationship? Remember now, this is about the relationship, not your ex. In other words, watch sentences that start with "He did…" or "He used to", etc. Good examples might be things like, "We never went on date nights alone together" or "We were always financially struggling" or "We spent all of our holidays with his family and barely any time with mine." Whatever it is, make sure it's about the relationship – the two of you – not just him.

7. Your Ex's Negative Qualities

Finally right? Write down the negative qualities of your ex. If you're currently in a phase of glorifying him because you want him back, this might be tough but be honest with yourself. We all have negative qualities and you need to write his down.

8. Positives that Became Negatives

Sometimes, people have qualities that look positive but, at some point, they turn negative. For example, I knew a guy once who, on the surface, looked like he was very caring toward his girlfriends, but what would happen later was that he would become obsessive and would want to know what they were doing all of the time. This is unhealthy behavior that, at first, might come off as cute or sweet. Another example would be someone who comes off as being a neat, clean type of individual but over time, you see that they are obsessive about cleanliness and demand everything be spotless all of the time.

9. Early Warning Signs

Invariably, there are early warning signs in relationships which ultimately come to an end. Looking back, what were the early warning signs for you? Maybe you saw flashes of anger, but not directed at you. Did these signs give you any indication that he would treat you badly or hurt you deeply? What did you do about it at the time? Did you rationalize it? How? Did you ignore it? What could you have done back then? Why didn't you take that action? What types of bargains did you make with yourself to make this okay? What compromises in your own values did you make to continue to allow him in your life?

10. Hurtful Incidents

Make a list of the top 5 most hurtful incidents in your relationship. What happened? What was done or said, or not done/said? Did anyone apologize? Did anyone promise not to let it happen again? Did it happen again? Were promises or apologies not kept or broken?

11. What did You Do?

Write about things you did wrong in the relationship. This isn't a list of what other people, including your ex, said you did wrong but what you know you did wrong, in your own heart. Were there things you did or did not do? Were there things you said or should have said? Did you have temper tantrums or were you too controlling? Did you check out or spend too much time with your friends and not enough with him?

12. *Issues From Your Behavior*

What major incidents happened as a result of your behavior or issues? Did you do or say something that led to a big fight? Did you not do things you should have, causing an argument? Looking at your list from the last exercise, what was the result of those things?

13. *Things Unsaid*

Often, we regret not saying something to someone. Are there things you wish you had said to your ex? If you could sit your ex down in a room with you right now, knowing he could not respond, what would you say? Think of anything that hasn't been covered in the other exercises of this inventory. What would you like to say now that you haven't yet written down?

After You Take A Break ...

After you have taken a break for a few days, revisit all of your answers. Some things will stand out as not being that important while other things will stand out as a big deal. Take notes as you read through and note the big deal items. If it was really important, write it down. Again, I've got a worksheet for you here: www.wholds

thecardsnow.com/hes-gone-now-what-downloads/. Use it or don't, your choice!

Similarly, if things on the list aren't as big of a big deal as others, you can cross them off. You can highlight the big deal items or rewrite them on your new page. This is your list to do what you want. If you find you've forgotten something important, it's okay to add it now. Rereading this may trigger things you didn't recall before. That's okay.

Your new list of things that were important might include some of the following types of items:

- How it feels to lose the positive things about him or the relationship

- How it feels to lose the negative things about him or the relationship

- What you are angry or hurt over

- What you will miss about him or the relationship

- What you want to say "Thank you" to him for

- What you want to say "I'm sorry" for

- Anything significant about the relationship

Write a letter

Now, it's time to write a letter to your ex. You are not going to send it. This is for your healing process. It is not for him. There is one key element that must be in your letter in order for it to promote healing for you. You need to include in this letter what you forgive your ex for.

Let's take a quick detour into why you need to forgive him because I can hear you groaning and pushing back from here.

Why Do You Need To Forgive?

Everyone thinks that when you forgive someone, you are saying that what they did was okay. That isn't what forgiveness is about. Let's first look at what forgiveness is not:

- Forgiveness is not condoning what someone did

- Forgiveness is not forgetting, which may not even be possible

- It doesn't meant that what happened is okay if it isn't

Forgiveness is about taking the negativity out of a situation. It is for you. It is about telling your mind that you are ready to move past this and begin healing. Most importantly, forgiveness is really you forgiving yourself.

What Happens To You When You Forgive?

- Hanging onto anger hurts you, not the person you need to forgive; forgiveness begins your growth

- You give yourself permission to live in the here and now, rather than in the past, which is where you live when you're constantly reliving the hurtful events

- You are able to move forward in your life without contempt, anger or the desire to get revenge

- You regain your power; when you are angry or resentful toward someone, they hold the power in your life – many say you allow that person to live rent-free in your head

- Your mental and physical health improve because the negativity that was bogging down the systems of your body is removed – if you don't believe me, re-visit the chapters in Phase 1 where we talked about the negative impacts on your body from stress You are once again able to see the positive traits of the person you were angry with, which enables you to accept that person for who they are; this doesn't mean you're ready to launch a new relationship with them but you are able to take all of the necessary steps to move forward

When you write your letter and include a statement which begins with, "I forgive..." you're telling yourself you have permission to move forward. You don't need to forgive him for everything but pick something you can let go of and start there.

Before you write the letter, make sure you've narrowed your list to just the important items. Choose those which you really feel strongly about and include them in your letter. Your last line should be your line of forgiveness. Also, write as if the other person is going to read it. Use full sentences. Don't include bullet points or acronyms and shorthand.

Once the letter is written, set it aside for a few days.

It is worth noting that if you have other relationships which are still haunting you, you can use this same Relationship Inventory for those. You follow all of the same steps, including writing the letter. Don't do them all in one day. Take your time and do these one at a time. Resolve one relationship before you tackle another. You will feel significantly better once you've completed this process.

Chapter 10

Taking Inventory 2— The Life Inventory

When we find ourselves in bad relationship after bad relationship, it damages our self-esteem and our confidence level drops. The more these two things drop, the more broken your process to choose a quality man becomes. Your chooser is broken. You probably get too deep into a relationship too quickly. You may allow a man to have sex with you too soon. You may feel as if you're in love way before you really are.

When you do a Life Inventory, you are giving yourself permission to take an honest look at your life and what you need to change. This isn't about calling yourself a failure or using any type of negative self-talk. This is about looking for areas which require positive change and formulating a plan to make that change. This is you giving yourself permission to change the patterns which have led you to make wrong choices in your relationship partners. This is different from the Relationship Inventory, which examined specific relationships and positioned you to let go of the pain they caused. With that done, we need to break the pattern. I have this entire process in one document for you here: www.whoholds thecardsnow.com/hes-gone-now-what-downloads/.

The Life Inventory

1. Look for patterns

Return to the Relationship Inventory you did for your most recent relationship. Take a new piece of paper or use the worksheet you just downloaded. On your paper, draw two lines down the middle vertically. At the top of one column, write "Negatives" and write "Positives" at the top of the next and write "Name" at the top of the last. One by one, look at each positive trait. Think back to other relationships you had and recall whether or not any of those men had those same traits. Write a name, or more than one name, in the "Name" column. Do the same for the negative traits. You're looking for patterns. There may be other people in your life, other than the men you were in relationships with, that you can look at as well – friends, family, peers.

2. Make a new list

Now, look for the patterns you uncovered and write them on a new sheet of paper. It's noteworthy if you have a trait which contains the names of all or most of the people you considered in completing the worksheet.

3. Let's look at Mom

Don't start cursing at me, just follow along and trust the process. Make a list of the positive and negative qualities of your Mom. After you make that list, go back and look at your list of traits from Step 1. How many people on your list have those same positive and negative traits?

4. Let's look at Dad

Do the same thing with your Dad.

5. Did you have other caretakers?

If you had other caretakers, like a grandparent, nanny or babysitter who had a significant influence in your life, do the same steps for those persons as well

As you can see, we are slowly but steadily working through all of your relationships and cross-referencing the positive and negative traits. Again, we are looking for patterns in your relationships.

6. What's my struggle?

If you're using your own paper, draw a line vertically down the center of your paper. At the top of one column, write "Negative traits I'm drawn to" and at the top of the other, write "Struggle I'm trying to overcome". We are usually drawn to people who fit narratives or past incidents or behaviors in our lives. If you had someone in your life who was abusive to you, you may choose abusers. This

could be a parent or relative, but it could also be a class-
mate or friend

Why Is This Helpful?

No relationship is healthier than its sickest partner.
Another way to say this is water seeks its own level. Either
way, what I'm saying is that you are no better off than the
worst-off person in your life. If you have people in your
life who wallow in self-pity or put others down, they are
not healthy people and you will ultimately drag yourself
down, even if it's not permanently, to their level.

If you recall, we talked about your brain and how it
manages information. Constant exposure to this type of
behavior only helps to stuff it into your brain deeper.

In order to build healthy relationships, we must sur-
round ourselves with healthy people. Yes, this means you
may need to swap out some friends or spend less time
with some family members. This is not easy and it isn't
fun, but you are working toward becoming a healthier
woman and that means you have tough choices to make.

If the person your Life Inventory keeps pointing to is
a parent, you can complete my Parent Inventory. That
inventory is the next chapter. Now that you can see the
behaviors or traits of the wrong men, you can recognize
red flags in new men you meet. You should be keenly

aware of the patterns of your past, which is good because we cannot break a pattern we cannot recognize.

Chapter 11

Taking Inventory 3— The Parent Inventory

This inventory is most useful if you found that your choices in men seem to be related to something you found relating to one parent or the other. You don't need to do this inventory for both parents unless both showed up in your analysis of why you choose the men you do. You can find a downloadable worksheet here: www.who-holdsthecardsnow.com/hes-gone-now-what-downloads/.

The Parent Inventory

1. *Do you wish you could change your parent?*

Often, we wish we could change people and our parents are no exception. Write down anything you wish you could change about the parent you're focusing on. Are there times when you felt disappointed by your parent? Did this parent ever embarrass you? Were there times when you felt this parent was not there for you as s/he should have been? Did this parent miss special events like plays, concerts or sporting events? How was this parent not quite the parent you needed him or her to be?

2. *Negative treatment by this parent?*

In your one-on-one relationship with this parent, were there ways in which s/he treated you in a negative way? Were you treated differently than your siblings? How did your two personalities just not mesh well together?

3. *Attempts to please him or her*

Often, when we perceive our relationship with a parent to be lacking something, we will look for ways to try to overcompensate by going out of our way to please him or her. Were there times where you went out of your way to please this parent but your efforts didn't work? Was it never enough with this parent?

4. *Rebel with a cause*

Many kids rebel against their parents and it can be normal, but if your relationship with this parent was on tenuous footing, your rebellion was sending a signal. Did you rebel against this parent? What did you do and what was his or her response?

5. *Pieces of the positive relationship*

No relationship is 100% positive or negative. There are always pieces of both. In your relationship with this parent, what were the positives? Think back to times when you felt accepted or when you felt the approval of this parent.

6. *What was good?*

Was there a time or more than one time when this relationship was clicking? Did you reach a point where you felt like maybe there had been a change for the better? Were there good times or special times?

7. *Your parent and others*

How did your parent interact with others? Make a list of how this parent interacted with the other members of your immediate family – any siblings, your other parent, etc. Was his or her treatment of those people similar to what you experienced? Did you learn how to respond to this parent by watching the other parent? Did your other parent criticize this parent in conversations with you? Did you hear the other parent criticize this parent to others? If this happened, how did it make you feel?

8. *Wanting change*

Did you ever try to change behaviors in your parent? Children of alcoholics who recognize the problem may try to hide their alcohol, for example. If you didn't try to change their behaviors, was it because you thought they would change with time? Did you spend time wishing this parent would change? Did his or her treatment of you surprise you?

9. *Split personality*

Did your parent have sort of a Dr. Jekyll/Mr. Hyde thing going? Sometimes he or she could be sweet as pie, other times you didn't know what would set them off next. Did you find yourself splitting this parent into good and bad? What were the benefits and detriments of doing this?

10. *What you feel you did wrong*

Even though you were a child for some or most of this, were there things you felt you did wrong when interacting with this parent? Were there times when you acted disrespectfully or you were disobedient? Did you lie or sneak around? Did you hide things?

11. *Things left unsaid*

Are there things you wish you could say to this parent? Have things gone unsaid? Write down anything you feel has gone unsaid.

12. *Forgiven*

As with the relationship inventory, it's time to write a letter to this parent, making sure to include forgiveness. If you need to do so, reread the section on forgiveness. Remember that forgiveness isn't for the person you are forgiving, it is for you. Carrying anger toward a parent is detrimental to all aspects of your life. Let it go with forgiveness.

Treat this inventory like the others, do it over the space of a few days or even a couple of weeks then walk away from it for a few days. This work is brutal and may bring up some bad memories. Feel the feelings that arise as you're completing this inventory. Stop and cry or go punch a pillow to get rid of what you're feeling. Work through the feelings, do not avoid or stuff them.

One More Thing Before You Go

There is just one more thing you need to do before we exit Phase 2 – I want you to officially let go of your past relationship. This is a symbolic letting go of the relationship, but it has proven to be quite helpful for many people who need to let go of past hurt.

Read the letter out loud.

If you have a friend or family member who is great at listening, ask them to listen while you read. If there is nobody you want to share it with, that's okay but it helps to have someone to listen. When you read the letter, don't rush through it. Read it slowly and carefully, allowing yourself to hear the words. Allow any feelings of sadness or anger to come. Stop if you need to collect yourself. Do not stuff the feelings or push them off for later. Feel them as they come.

Burn it.

Now, burn the letter. Please be careful – don't toss it in your gas fireplace or burn it in a trash can. Find a safe way to burn it. As you do, you need to say something very similar to this: "Thank you [name of ex] for being a part of my life. I am now letting you go with love."

Don't roll your eyes or shout "NO WAY!" at me right now. This is for you, remember. This is the healthy way to let go. Even if you don't really feel very loving toward your ex right now, this isn't really about him, it's about you and you're healthier now than you were when we began this journey. You need to do this in a loving way for your own sake, not for his.

Walk away.

Once the letter is burned and all flames are safely out, dispose of the remains and walk away. Again, this is a healthy way of finishing the letting go process. You are physically and emotionally walking away from the relationship. It is in your past. It now just symbolizes healthy lessons you learned about yourself and the positives from the relationship. You've forgiven and you have let go with love.

Feel free to do this same letting go process with the other letters you have written during this process. It is very therapeutic to go through the ritual. While it is symbolic, many feel a lot of freedom from doing it.

Now, it's time to move on!

PHASE 3
Building Your
Post-Relationship Life

By now, you should be feeling better about things. If you aren't, revisit the activities in the previous chapters and reread the stages of grief. See where you are and define the tactics you can work on again to help you feel ready.

In this last phase of your recovery, we are going to be moving toward a new relationship, a new you. This is the phase where we create a healthy definition of relationship and of love. This is the phase where you learn to be a confident individual so you can be an excellent partner in your new relationship. This is where the magic of moving on begins! I'm excited for you!

Chapter 12

Where Does Happiness Come From?

All too often, I hear women say, "I can't be happy without him" or "I can't be happy if I don't have a man in my life". This makes me cringe because it tells me that the person I'm trying to help doesn't understand where happiness comes from.

The truth about happiness is this - the only people seeking happiness are those who don't have it. Much like someone who has confidence doesn't think about confidence, someone who is happy doesn't think about being happy. They just are happy.

Why am I harping on this today?

Because you need to have a complete understanding of where happiness comes from before you embark on another relationship! You will be happy when you are living your life according to your values. Not someone else's values – yours. You will be happy when you have figured out who your ideal self is and you are living your life as that person. You will be happy when you are pursuing hobbies and passions that interest you. You will be happy when you are pursuing your goals and dreams – and achieving those goals.

Finding someone to fill a void in your life is like pouring water into a bucket with a hole in the bottom. You won't ever fill that void in that way because that isn't really what caused it. If you feel empty, then you aren't living according to your values. You're not your ideal self. You're bored because you sit at home all day, every day worrying about one thing or another, rather than going out and finding something to interest you.

Your happiness comes from inside you. It comes from living your life in harmony with the things you believe in. It comes from surrounding yourself with people who have those same values. It comes from pursuing goals which line up with those values. Never, ever does it come from having a man in your life.

When you think happiness is coming from outside, you are confusing it with pleasure. We seek pleasure in a variety of ways. Sometimes it comes from spending time with someone special. Sometimes it comes from doing something you love. Sometimes it comes from giving or serving someone in need. Pleasure can come from many directions but it isn't the same thing as being happy. Happiness is a way of being. It's a state of mind. Pleasure is an experience. Much like failure is about an event and not the person involved in the event, pleasure is an experience, not a state of mind. It's temporary. Think of it this way – a drug addict finds pleasure in the next hit but I guarantee you he's not happy.

Let's try another way to understand it. Think about a time when you were really angry. Are you thinking in that moment, "Am I really angry?" or "Am I doing this right?" No. You're angry, you're not worried about whether or not you're really angry or if you're doing angry right. You're fired up and that's what matters. It's a state of being. So is happiness. If you're happy, you're not thinking, "Am I happy?" You just are happy.

Happiness Isn't About Success

In the same way that happiness isn't about having a man in your life, it's not about being successful either. I can guarantee you that there are tons of people who, by your own standards, are successful but they're not happy. Happiness doesn't come from your achievements. It doesn't come from being dressed in the right outfit or from wearing the right shoes. Happiness is a state of being which comes from, as I stated previously, living your life in harmony with your values and beliefs. If you're not happy, you're not living your life in tune with what you believe in, at your core. This, we can fix!

Happiness Isn't About Always Being Positive

You know this person and you've probably wanted to slap them at least once in your life. It's the always positive, always upbeat person. This is the Suzy Sunshine of the office who always puts a positive spin on anything. She smiles when she tells you she just came from a root canal. Don't let her fool you – that's the anesthesia talking. Her face is just numb!

Yes, in order to be happy, you should have a positive out-look, but life isn't all sunshine and rainbows. If I'm the first to tell you this, sorry for not warning you first. It is okay to get angry. It is okay to feel sad. It is even okay to want to punch someone – of course actually punching them is not okay, but the desire is fine.

What many people don't understand and what brings a lot of folks down is the belief that you shouldn't feel neg-ative emotions. You shouldn't cry. You shouldn't ever get mad. Even if you believe in non-violence, you're still gonna get mad sometimes. It's just the nature of being a human being with feelings. The trick is to allow those feelings to come and to become comfortable feeling them.

When you get angry, it's hard to just stop and evalu-ate, but if you are in control of your emotions and your thoughts, you can manage it. Have you ever been in the car and someone pulls out in front of you, cutting you off? Of course you have. What's your response? You flip them the bird and start shouting obscenities right? Me too, but the difference is I quickly reel it in and say, "Gregg, cool down. That guy is a jerk but there's no good to come from being so mad." Make a choice in how you react. We'll talk more about this later. My point is clear – allow yourself to feel what you feel but also allow yourself to recognize the emotion and put a stop to the potentially harmful feelings you have. Get comfortable feeling pain. It will still suck but you'll learn that it will pass. Get comfortable experiencing failure. We all fail, there is no way to stop it so just get comfortable with it.

Happiness Comes From Being Your Ideal Self

We are about to dig into this a little deeper, but you need to know that you will be happy when you are living your life true to who you are. That probably wasn't true in your past relationship. You may be saying to yourself, "But Gregg, who am I?" We're going to figure that out next. For now, trust me when I say you have all of these components in your life already. You just haven't yet recognized them or known what to do with them. That's why you have your trusty coach, Gregg, here to help you!

Who is your ideal you?

There is a version of you we will call your ideal you or your ideal self. This is the person you want to become. This isn't about what you want to have or what you want to achieve as much as it is about who you are inside. This version of you is a reflection of your values. You define integrity based on how you define your ideal self.

This seems difficult to understand but it's not as hard as it sounds. This breaks down into how you manage things like relationships with others, how you manage conflict, how you handle yourself at work or at home, etc. Your ideal self at work will be defined somewhat differently than how you define your ideal self with your significant other. Let's look at some examples.

As an ideal girlfriend, I will show my boyfriend I care for him with my words, my actions and my attention.

As an ideal manager, I will show the people who work under me that I value them by being an attentive listener and making time to hear their concerns.

As an ideal mother, I will be supportive of their hopes and dreams and will provide them with the tools possible to pursue those things.

Your ideal self may need some work but that's okay. That's what we're going to do now. When you begin to identify and work toward your ideal self, people will notice. The first step in working on your ideal self is to identify your values. Values can be tricky but we're going to make it easier.

How do values and your ideal self go together?

If you value being healthy, not wasting food and exercise, part of your ideal self should reflect the healthy person you value. This means thinking more carefully about what you eat, what you buy and how active you are. If you're a smoker, it means quitting. If you drink a lot, it means going on the wagon. Any activity which doesn't align with your healthy value will cause you some issues.

Your ideal self is also reflected in the people you hang out with. If your friends all like to go out on Saturday nights and get drunk and you tag along, it says something about what you value and your ideal self. If you opt to stay home and hang out with them when they're doing something else, that is also a statement.

If you have zero dollars in your bank account but go out to buy a new car, it speaks to your ideal self. The question you need to ask is how are the things you do lining up with your ideal self? You need to become more mindful of your actions in order to live in harmony with the person you want to become. Healing from your breakup and moving on means making some changes and this is your moment. Today is the day you figure out who you really want to portray to the world and how the things you do reflect that version of yourself.

Survival Tactic #12

I want to encourage you not to get online and look for a list of values. They exist, but all this will do is cause you to pick the ones which feel the most like you. Your values need to be uncovered by you, not picked from a list. Stay with me and I'll help you figure them out. If you would like to download a worksheet, click here: www.whoholdsthecardsnow.com/hes-gone-now-what-downloads/.

First and foremost, know that you will follow your values without thinking about it in times of stress, so the first way to figure out your values is to take a look at how you may have reacted in times of stress or in an emergency. When faced with a choice of doing one thing or another, your values drove you to choose what you did.

Next, think of times where you felt the happiest. What were you doing? Where were you? Who were you with? What values were you honoring at that time? Maybe you received an award at work for punctuality or not missing a day. Maybe you just received your diploma and were honored with a scholarly award of some sort. In that event, you may have been honoring your value of hard work, dedication or integrity.

Now let's go in a different direction. Think of a time where you were really angry, upset or frustrated. What was going on? Where were you? Who were you with?

What emotion were you feeling? Now, what is the opposite emotion? An opposite emotion would be gratification or satisfaction. What about that particular incident made you feel you were not satisfied? What was missing? If someone cuts you off while you're driving, for example, you were angry with them because they weren't being courteous or kind. Maybe you were frustrated because they didn't allow you to take your turn – they weren't being fair to you. You will find a suppressed value in the emotion opposite to what you're feeling.

Think about things which are very important to you in your life. What is your personal code of conduct? For example, do you feel it is rude to be late to a meeting? Do you feel it is inconsiderate not to respond to a text, email or phone call right away? Do you get annoyed with people who don't shake your hand or greet you kindly when you meet? How do you behave in certain situations? Your personal behavior will tell you a lot about what you value.

Finally, look at the things which interest you. Are you a creative person? Maybe you're more introspective or inquisitive. Do you enjoy music or looking at art? You could value creativity, curiosity, innovation, ingenuity or even those things themselves – art, music, etc.

Make your list as you answer these questions. The answers become your overall list of values but we're not quite done yet. Next, your job is to group these under similar themes. For example, you may have said you value creativity, innovation and ingenuity. You can group these into one category. If you had honesty and integrity, you can group those together. Your first list, after answering the questions above, should contain about 20-40 terms, maybe more. By the time you group them down, you should have significantly fewer. After you have them grouped, it's time to find a central theme for each group. Honesty, transparency, integrity, truth and directness can all go under one umbrella which you can label with any one of those words – integrity probably fits best. Do this for each group.

Now, look at your list. You may still have a lot of groups and that's okay. The important thing now is to determine which ones are the primary values of your life. Which ones define who you are, not who someone else wants you to be but who you are? Those are your core values. Those are your go-to's when you need to make a snap decision on how to behave in a specific situation or how to react to something. The ones you didn't put into the primary group can sit in what we'll call a secondary group for now.

At this point, allow these to sit. Sleep on them. Revisit them in a day or two and then reevaluate. Are these still right or do you need to maybe move one from the primary list back to your secondary list? Don't force this.

You need to take time to really make sure you've nailed the list. It's possible you may sleep on it and think of things you left off of your original list. That's okay. You shouldn't expect yourself to get this right on the first try. It's too important to place that kind of pressure on the activity. This could take you days or even weeks to flesh out. Allow yourself that time.

Once you're happy with your list, it's time to have a little fun. You want to turn your values into emotionally-based statements which will resonate with you. Your goal is to write statements which will root into your unconscious mind, which means they need to evoke strong positive emotion in you. "I value health". What you might want to say instead is something like "I value living my life with full energy and vitality every day". This is a statement you can get behind. This is something which should stir at least a little positive emotion in you. If you said you value honesty, don't just say, "I value honesty". Say something like, "It is important to me to conduct my life with the utmost honesty." These statements are more personal. Your brain will not be excited by something mundane like 'I value honesty" or a simple list, "Honesty, health, creativity, …" Your subconscious will reject this list as boring and it will never make it any further than your conscious mind.

Your final step is to repeat these statements to yourself and make sure they make you feel good, excited even.

These need to stir your emotions. This is necessary for them to root down into your unconscious.

Returning to Your Ideal Self
Who do you admire?

Another way to identify what your ideal self looks like is to examine the lives of a couple of people you admire. This can be someone you know personally, or someone who is a celebrity or is well-known. What are the things about those people which appeal to you? Why do you admire this person?

Doing this helps you to get a handle on what traits you want to have in your ideal self and also how you define success. It also helps you to look at character traits other people have so you can figure out what you want to develop in yourself. You want to examine how this person acts when they're around others. How do they treat their friends and family?

I recently heard a story about Gene Wilder. After fellow actor Marty Feldman passed away, Wilder contacted his wife to ask if they owned their home. She responded that they did not. He replied with, "Well now you do" and bought the home for her so she had somewhere to live now that her husband was gone. That speaks a lot about the character of Gene Wilder and that is a trait I would like to have in myself.

Also, look at how this person acts in public. If it's someone close to you, you have probably had ample opportunity to take note of this. What is it about the way this person acts that appeals to you? What do you want people to think about you when they see you or experience time with you?

Survival Tactic #13

I have a worksheet for this exercise for you here: www. whoholdsthecardsnow.com/hes-gone-now-what-downloads/.

Write down 3 people you admire. They can be someone famous or someone you know personally. Write down what it is about them which causes you to admire them. Some celebrities are outspoken on certain causes, like animal or human rights. Others are more politically outspoken or have a specific set of values relating to sexual values, spiritual values, etc. Make a list of what it is about that person that so intrigues you. These are traits which are important to you. These are hints at who you want your ideal self to be.

Chapter 13
Boundaries

It's time to have the inevitable discussion about boundaries. In Phase 2, we talked about strengthening your resolve to keep conversations to the business of your current relationship – the kids, your shared financial assets and your workplace and if you don't share those things, you avoid all contact with him.

You just spent a significant amount of time working on some of the inventories from Phase 2. Now, we need to have a preliminary discussion about boundaries. In order to move forward in a healthy way, you need to have a full understanding of boundaries and where you may need to set them in your life.

What Are Boundaries?

Boundaries can be most easily thought of as where you begin and where someone else ends. I suppose that isn't so easy so let's look at it another way. A boundary is a space or a limit you place between you and someone else. Think of it as a fence you place to separate acceptable treatment of you from unacceptable treatment.

When I write my dating books, I often talk about your need for boundaries in dating. What I mean when I say this is that you need to use your values to create rules about how people treat you. It means you don't let a man convince you to have sex with him on a first date. It means you look at your values, which we just uncovered in the last chapter, and you establish a set of standards for how people will treat you.

Let's look at an example. Debbie and Susan are friends but Susan is always running late and Debbie likes to be on time. They meet with some of their friends once a week to hang out. Susan usually drives and picks Debbie up at her house but she's always late. Debbie has two choices. She can set a boundary with Susan or she can continue to be late.

Debbie decides, with the help of her therapist, to set a boundary with Susan. She calls Susan to confirm their plans for the upcoming night out. Before Debbie hangs up, she tells Susan, "I'll be ready at 8. If you're running late, I'll just go ahead by myself." When the night out comes, Debbie waits patiently until 8:00. At 8, Debbie gets a text from Susan, "I'll be there in a few minutes." Debbie texts back, "No need. I will go on ahead without you." Susan argues back, "No, wait for me. I'll be there in less than 10." Debbie repeats her statement, "I'll go ahead without you" and Susan comes back once more, "Please wait for me Debbie – less than 10 I promise!" At this point, Debbie ends the conversation by saying, "I'll see you at the restaurant."

Debbie set a boundary with Susan, and if you were paying attention, you noticed that Debbie also used the rule of 3 to hold tight to her boundary. What happens next?

It's possible that when Susan got to the event, she treated Debbie poorly. She may have ignored her or maybe she berated her in front of their friends. This is an attempt to make Debbie feel badly for holding to the boundary she set with Susan. If Debbie gives Susan time, and holds to her boundaries, odds are Susan will come around but regardless of whether Susan comes around or not, Debbie has to realize that she stuck to her boundaries and Susan is making a choice of how she reacts to them. When you enforce boundaries, it is important to remember that your happiness matters. You are enforcing a boundary to hold tight to your own values.

When someone reacts negatively to your boundaries, that's on them. Setting boundaries is meant to help you navigate your life and avoid being used or abused by others. In your future relationships, having boundaries will be very important in maintaining the confidence you're rebuilding and sticking to your values. People who do not respect your boundaries or people who punish you after you establish boundaries probably need to be let go from your life. If it's a family member, you may need to cut back the amount of time you spend with that person.

How Do You Set Healthy Boundaries?

Observe and determine where you need boundaries.

You might not be aware of where you need to set boundaries so you need to become a bit of a detective in your own life. What this means is that you need to make some observations about how you feel in different situations.

- What makes you angry?

- When do you get frustrated?

- When do you feel hurt?

- Do you feel someone has taken advantage of you?

- Do you feel disrespected?

These are all signals your boundaries are being crossed and you need to look at how you can set a boundary to alleviate those negative feelings.

Allow time.

Setting boundaries is not a speedy process. You didn't get to a place where this person took advantage of you overnight. There was a pattern of behavior which led up to this point. In addition, you will need to summon the courage and resolve to set boundaries and stick to them. The first time Debbie told Susan she would go ahead without her, Susan may have gotten angry but she may not have fully gotten the message. The same thing may have occurred the following week. It may have taken 2 or three times of Debbie leaving without Susan before she really got the message and started showing up on time.

Communication effectively.

One key to setting healthy boundaries is to communicate effectively. It is important to use "I" statements, instead of "You" statements. Sentences which begin with "you" indicate blame while sentences which begin with "I" tell the other person you are expressing your feelings about something. Let's look at the difference.

"You always make me late for work because you can't get out of bed on time"

Or

"I get frustrated when I am late to work all of the time"

Which one would you be more responsive to? Most people would rather hear the second statement and would be more open to a discussion.

Be honest.

Sometimes, it is very hard to be honest with our loved ones about our own feelings. It makes us feel guilty so we tiptoe around what we want to say instead of just coming out with it. When you can't express your true feelings about something, you're not telling someone what your boundaries are. I know it will be difficult to speak honestly about your feelings if you're not accustomed to doing so, but it's something you're going to have to do if you want to move forward and be a more confident woman.

Allow for consequences.

There are two types of consequences, natural and logical. Natural consequences are consequences which happen without your intervention. For example, if a child pokes around in the morning and doesn't get ready when he's told to, he will be late for school. Of course, you could bail him out and take him so he's on time but then, he won't learn anything about his behavior. That is a natural consequence. In relationships, we often insulate our loved ones from consequences, even if it's at our own expense. Your ex may have had a drug or drinking problem that you excused away or covered with your own actions.

In order to have consequences, you may need to issue a warning like this, "If you don't get ready for school, you're going to be late." Your next move is to hold tight to your warning and not bail out your child. This isn't the same as threatening someone. If a child doesn't do his or her homework, he will get a failing grade for it. That's a natural consequence. If your boyfriend drinks all the time, you stop calling his work to make excuses for him, "Jim is home sick today." You let him get fired. Allowing natural consequences to occur is not fun, but you need to do it regardless.

Our example of Debbie and Susan above is an example of logical consequences. You tell someone, if A happens, you will do B. You must be able to follow through as Debbie did. Remember in our example, Debbie didn't say "You're always late. If you're late tonight I will go without you." Instead, Debbie said, "I'll be ready at 8. If you're not here, I will go ahead by myself". It would have been okay even for Debbie to have said, "I don't like being late to meet with our friends all of the time."

When you are talking about consequences, you are giving the other person a choice. If you do X, Y will happen. This is true of either natural or logical consequences.

Be brief.

You don't need to provide a big, detailed explanation for your boundary. When you are laying out the consequence, you need to be as brief as possible. "If you're not here by 8, I will just go ahead without you." It's not long and drawn out.

When you set a boundary, the person you're setting it with will often ask for an explanation. You do not need to explain. You don't need to clarify your position. Chances are, however, this is what you're accustomed to doing. What you also don't do is lie. Let's look at an example again.

Emily and Jen have been friends for several years but during that time, Jen has pushed Emily around, invalidated her feelings and treated her disrespectfully. After seeking therapy for her low self-esteem, Emily decided it was time to put an end to being treated poorly. Jen was having a party, something she did often and Emily usually went but this time, she decided she would not go. Her urge was to lie to Jen and tell her she had somewhere else to go but her therapist encouraged her to simply be brief. Emily simply told Jen that she was not coming. Emily had to resist the urge to provide an explanation to Jen. Her therapist had warned her that Jen would ask for, even demand an explanation. Emily simply said, "I'm sorry Jen, I cannot attend." She left it at that. It was difficult for her but she did it.

You must do the same. A boundary crasher wants you to give an explanation so they can argue with it or debunk it. The truth is you don't owe anyone an explanation for holding to your boundaries.

This is going to suck at first.

Setting boundaries, at first, is not fun. It is going to make you feel uneasy and uncomfortable. The only way through this feeling is straight through – forward. In other words, you're going to have to power through, feel uncomfortable and realize that each time you do it, it will get a little easier.

Each time you do it, you should feel a little bit of self-esteem return. You should begin to feel more confident each time you stand up for yourself.

This is powerful stuff!

Choose your battles.

When you are setting boundaries, you don't need to go full on and tackle everything at once. After you've completed your observations and you know where boundaries need to be set, look the list over and pick two or three to work on first. Which boundaries are bothering you the most? Those are the ones you want to tackle first. Understand why you are choosing to set that boundary so you are clear and firm in setting it and standing up for yourself.

Mean what you say.

If you set a boundary and then give in to someone who tries to crash your boundary, your credibility is as good as gone. When you set a boundary, you need to be prepared to stand behind what you say. When Debbie told Susan she was going to leave at 8 if she wasn't there, the best thing she could have done is to leave at 8, as promised. If she had waited until Susan got there, she wouldn't have been able to get Susan to show up on time or believe her ultimatum again if she tried to set it. If you say you're going to do something, or not do something, that's what you must stand by.

This isn't about their feelings, it's about yours

People pleasers do so because they don't want to hurt someone's feelings. They say yes to keep the peace. When you begin to set boundaries, you may feel as if you're going to hurt the boundary crashers feelings.

You setting boundaries is about you holding true to your own values. It is not about someone else's feelings. You may not like knowing someone is angry with you but you must learn how to sit with these feelings and get comfortable in it. Again, as you do this more and more, it will get easier and you will come to realize one important fact. The boundary crasher did not care about your feelings when they pushed you beyond acceptable limits and now, you need to take care of yourself. You cannot hold true to your own values and worry about someone else's feelings at the same time. What you should be asking yourself is why this person doesn't care about your feelings.

If that doesn't work for you, think of it this way – saying yes to one thing means you're saying no to something else. Saying yes to allowing someone to crash your boundaries means saying no to your own values.

Prepare.

Before you set a boundary with someone, especially the first few times, you must prepare in advance. This may sound silly, but it will help. Let's imagine that your sister always insists you shop together but she always forces her own choice on you and it's usually a gift you know your mother either doesn't need or won't like.

This year, you decide you're not going to go shopping with your sister. You're just going to get your own gift. In order to prepare in advance for this boundary, you need to practice. Prepare your own words first. When she calls to set up your annual shopping trip, what will you say? Play the conversation in your head, or even better, write it out and say it out loud. Like everything else, the more senses you use the more real it will become.

Your Sister: "Hey! When do you want to go shopping for Mom's birthday? I can do either Saturday or Sunday. What works for you?"

You: "Actually, I am just going to get Mom a gift myself this year."

Your sister: "What? Seriously? But we always go in together to get Mom something. Come on – go with me. Don't break tradition!"

At this point, you might be tempted so here is where you need to really practice.

You: "No, I'm just going to get Mom a gift myself."

Your Sister: "I can't believe you're doing this to me! You know how much fun we always have shopping together! What is your problem?!?!?!"

You: "I really need to run. I'll see you at the party!"

Get a friend to play your sister and prompt her about what to say. If you find someone who knows your sister, even better because she may be able to play the role without prompting. Any preparation you can get in before you actually speak with your sister will help you get through it.

Always remember you have three goals – to hold true to your own values, to avoid answering any questions and to stick to your guns. Do not give in.

Survival Tactic #14

It's time to begin setting boundaries. First, observe where you feel your boundaries might be broken. Reread that part of this chapter so you know how to go about it. After you have your list of which boundaries are being broken, start writing out how you will begin to enforce those boundaries. Remember, it will be challenging to tackle them all at once. Choose the ones which are really important first and work on those. Take the steps outlined in the chapter above to begin your boundary setting journey. This won't be easy but you must stick with it! I know you can do it! Would I leave you without a worksheet? Find yours for this exercise here: www.whoholdsthecardsnow.com/hes-gone-now-what-downloads/

Chapter 14

What is Love?

My friend, Dr. Helen Fisher, a behavioral anthropologist, has made it her life's work to study and understand romantic love, mate choice, marriage, adultery and all things associated with love. I have found perhaps the clearest definition of love on her website, The Anatomy of Love. She breaks the brain systems relating to romantic relationships down into three systems: lust, romantic love and attachment. Dr. Fisher's results are the result of studying our brains in these different systems. Our brains look different in lust, romantic love and attachment.

Three Systems of The Brain

1. *Lust*

Before we define what love is, let's take a quick look at what love is not. Love is not lust. This is your sex drive, which Dr. Fisher argues is part of our evolutionary past and is designed to help you seek a variety of potential partners. We are capable of having sex without feeling love and we are also capable of having a sex drive without being in love with a particular person.

Your sex drive can kick in when you are watching a movie or maybe a certain actor. It can kick in when you hear a certain song on the radio or see an image of someone who fits your ideal sex partner. Porn exists and thrives because we have a sex drive but we're not always in love. I'm not saying this makes porn okay, but that's why it's a big industry.

2. *Romantic love*

This is also called attraction when we're talking about your brain systems. This is where you have obsessive thinking about or a craving for a particular person. Note that distinction between lust and romantic love. There are others, but lust is not directed at one person in particular while romantic love is.

Romantic love evolved for humans so we can choose a partner to mate with. This is our primal need to procreate – to have children. For that, we need to feel a sexual drive toward someone, but we also need to feel attracted to them. People often mistake lust for the beginning of romantic love.

3. *Attachment*

In the attachment phase of a relationship, we feel a deep sense of connection to one person. Attachment is never the first step of a relationship. It evolves somewhere around 6 months after romantic love sets in but can take up to 2 years to form. This is the system of our brain which allows us to remain with our romantic love partner long enough to rear our children, and beyond. This is also the partner you care to be around, even though you have no plans to procreate. In other words, you will be okay staying with this person after your children have grown because of the deep attachment.

What Does Romantic Love Feel Like?

Let's begin by talking about the first phase of love. We don't need to talk about lust or sex drive because we discussed boundaries previously and you know what you will and will not tolerate in that regard, and, that's not love. There do seem to be a few characteristics of romantic love we all share and experts can agree upon.

You crave him.

In this craving him place, you want him to call, you want him to text, you want to see and spend time with him. You want him to ask you out. When it comes time, you want him to tell you he loves you. You have this emotional craving for these things from this man and only this man.

You have obsessive thoughts.

We're talking obsessive in a healthy way, for the most part, here. You can't stop thinking about him. Your coworkers may find you staring at your computer screen, lost in your thoughts about him. This is also called intrusive thinking – it's so strong it can intrude on your life and take over your thoughts.

You will do anything to win him.

This is a huge one for men but it's true for both men and women. This is what I call 'the chase'. Men love to chase – they want to win you. Men are competitive and this speaks to their highly competitive nature. If a man is feeling romantic love, he will do what it takes to win you over and vice versa. This does not mean you set aside your boundaries but your mindset is "I want him and I'll do what it takes to win him over".

How Do You Know When You're In Love?

Many times, we mistake lust for love. We meet someone who fits our mental image of our ultimate sexual partner – our romantic and subsequently, our attachment love. While we may want to have sex with that person because he fits that image, he may not be the one. This is where many men and women make their first relationship mistake. This is why I always tell women to wait for a man to earn sex with them.

He is special.

When you are in love, you will begin to feel and see that he is unique. You won't have these feelings for anyone else but him. The scientific explanation for this is those happiness chemicals we talked about way back in the beginning of this book. Remember, we talked about how breaking the addiction to those chemicals is more difficult than breaking an addiction to crack?

Well, when you're feeling romantic love, you've got higher levels of dopamine, which is a chemical associated with attention and focus. Higher levels of dopamine mean higher attention and focus on your guy.

You've got rose-colored glasses.

Your friends may be wagging a finger at you, telling you to slow down, but in romantic love, you don't see his negatives. That's why we did the relationship inventory. It forces you to acknowledge the negatives you knew were there but weren't truly seeing at the time. You may focus on events you've attended together or the special things he has done for you and ignore any hurtful things he's done. You daydream about those wonderful circumstances.

This is still that dopamine hard at work – focus and attention all over again. Additionally, though, we're adding in some norepinephrine for good measure. This is a memory chemical so it helps you hang onto those positive memories longer.

You're on an emotional rollercoaster.

You may be feeling a plethora of things – excited, exhilarated, euphoric, high levels of energy, sleeplessness, a loss of appetite, maybe even some trembling, racing heart, anxiety, panic and feelings of despair.

Does this remind you of anyone you know? If you said no, congratulations – you don't know any drug addicts (or friends in love). These feelings are all a result of the chemicals…again. This might sound very similar to how you felt during the breakup, except in love, you'll feel more of the positive emotions and in the breakup, the predominance may be on the negative emotions.

Love is an addiction and you're hooked when you feel like this.

You've got intrusive thinking.

Remember in the last section, we talked about obsessive or intrusive thinking? This is a sign you're in love and it comes, most likely, from a decreased level of serotonin. For people who suffer from obsessive-compulsive disorder, treatment drugs which include serotonin are the best course because it helps to increase that level of serotonin in their brains.

You are emotionally dependent.

For better or worse, and right now, it's for worse, we become emotionally dependent on people we fall in love with, even after they have rejected us. MRI data shows the same reaction in the brains of people when they were shown someone they were in love with at the time of the study and someone they once loved but who had rejected them. This part of the brain is the part which controls cravings, so you're craving the other person. This comes out in the form of possessiveness, jealousy, fear of rejection and even separation anxiety.

As you can see, these are not healthy reactions to being in love, but nonetheless, they are reactions you can have. Become aware of them and recognize them as unhealthy.

You want to plan a future with him.

You may find yourself daydreaming about your future with your romantic love. This is equal to other survival urges we have, like the need for water and air. While you might be feeling this, it is important to make sure your guy feels the same way before you go having any future life talks. Men tend to cringe at these if they're not ready. Too much too fast can push him away.

You feel empathy toward him.

Empathy and sympathy are two different emotions. With empathy, you feel what they feel. With sympathy, you feel sorry for what they feel but you don't necessarily feel their pain. When you're experiencing romantic love, you feel empathy. If he hurts, you hurt. If he has suffered a tremendous loss, you may feel that loss as well. You also have a feeling that you are willing to sacrifice anything for him.

You want to be like him.

In my book, Night Moves, I talk about how you can make a guy fall in love with you by using synchronicity. You know you're in love with a guy when you want to be more like him. You may have an urge to dress more like him, change your priorities or even your values to align with his.

This is not a good idea!! I can't stress this enough. While creating a sense of synchronicity is a good thing, there is such a thing as too much. He is interested in you as you were when he met you, which was not a carbon copy of himself. If you go changing who you are, you're likely to push him further away. While sharing some things is a good idea, changing who you are to match up with your guy is not. Keep wearing the clothing you like. Keep your values right where they are. If you want to align or use synchronicity, mirror his actions or find a way to share a hobby with him, especially one he's interested in!

You want sexual exclusivity.

When you are in love, you don't want to have sex with anyone else. All of your lustful feelings and your sex drive is focused just on him and vice versa. Therefore, if he still wants to have sex with other women, that's your cue that he's not in love with you.

By the same token, if you don't feel the need to be exclusive with one man, you're simply feeling lust and not love.

Sex is not the most important thing.

In a healthy romantic love relationship, you want an emotional connection more than you want great sex. What this means is that, while the sex is good and you only want sex with him, you understand that intimacy comes from shared times, not sex, and you want to build that to a higher, stronger level.

In other words, in a lust situation, you won't want an emotional connection to form between you and your sex partner and vice versa. You're in it for the hookup, no strings attached.

Your passion is involuntary.

Have you ever had a crush on someone you knew you couldn't have? Maybe your boss or a coworker where fraternization is not allowed? Perhaps a celebrity – someone out of reach for you due to distance or some other restriction? Still, you feel love for this person and you can't seem to help it.

This is what it means to feel involuntary love toward someone. Yes, it can be directed at someone you're attracted to and you can have a relationship with as well. It just comes on as something you cannot control.

How Do You Know When You've Reached Attachment?

At some point, a good romantic relationship will reach the attachment phase but how do you know you're there?

Generally speaking, you lose the spark between you. At this point, you may slide into a healthy codependence. By this, I mean you're dependent on one another in a healthy way, not in a way which ultimately damages your relationship. Every relationship either ends up here, or it just plain ends.

Long distance relationships may stay in a romantic love phase longer because you aren't together as often, therefore it takes you longer to build intimacy and each time you're together, the newness of the relationship can kick in, keeping you sort of stuck there longer.

Chapter 15

How Do I Know
When I'm Ready for
a New Relationship?

This is a tough question to answer but one I know you're asking. I've coached women who want to jump right into another relationship after one ends and other women who have been bitten so many times that they can't imagine going through that pain again.

Single Isn't Bad!

First of all, let's dispel a myth. It is not bad to be single. While society tells us that being single means we're somehow damaged or unlovable, that simply isn't the truth. Once you are single and can embrace all of the benefits of being single, the danger becomes getting too comfy as a single woman. If you're happy with this, then fine. You don't need to read this last part of the book, but, if you want to enter into another relationship – a healthy relationship, then you need to embrace being single first.

Why do I need to be single at all?

We have already discussed the benefits of being single:

- You have time to grieve and process your feelings

- You get to know yourself again and determine what your own likes and wants are

- You can take a look at your values and really define them

- You have time to set healthy boundaries

- You learn how to do things for yourself, rather than relying on others

- You build your confidence through your independence and by having free time to explore new things

- You can write your story!

- You can explore new hobbies and passions and find some that are a fit for you

You, and only you, know when you're ready.

Don't let other people tell you you've been single long enough or that you're ready when you know you're not. Social pressure may make you want to find a boyfriend – all of your friends have boyfriends or husbands. You're the odd woman out with none.

Fine, enjoy living your life for yourself for a while. Just because they're all in relationships doesn't mean they're happier than you are. In fact, they may not be.

We all have some level of what we'll call dating energy. Yours may be pretty low right now. You've been in a relationship or two, maybe more, and you just went through one that ended. Each time a relationship ends, your dating energy is lower than it should be. The worse the breakup, the lower your energy after.

Along with low dating energy, you may feel kind of bitter toward men. This is normal but you can't let it last. What one man did to you is not indicative of what all men will do. You have to lose this bitterness before you re-enter the dating scene. Men can sniff out bitterness like they can beer and hot pizza and no man wants to date a man-hater.

Ask Yourself These Questions

There are thousands, heck probably millions of self-tests available online these days. Some may be reliable but most are crap. If you want a baseline for determining whether or not you're ready for a relationship, answer these questions:

1. Have you recovered fully from your last breakup?

2. Do you feel good enough about yourself to get back
    out there?

3. Are you really open to the possibilities in front of
    you?

4. Are you ready to look at your marketability?

5. Do you currently have available, potential options?

Answering positively to these 5 questions doesn't mean
you're ready per se, but it means you're on the right track.
As I said, only you will know.

What happens if you get out there and:

*   You panic and bail before you find someone

*   You find yourself bailing on what seem to be good
    guys

*   You can't seem to find a guy who's good enough

Each of these is a signal to you that you're not quite ready.
This isn't a bad thing. In fact, recognizing that you're not
quite ready is a very healthy thing to do because it shows
you're aware of yourself and what you're feeling. It also
helps you know where to begin.

You panic.

If you panic and bail, it may mean you're carrying some anxiety. You're worrying about negative things happening before you've even met someone. You may feel unworthy of a good man. This is your self-esteem telling you it's still in the tank or at least lower than we'd like to see it for dating. This doesn't mean you aren't datable, it makes you pretty close to normal. One in 14 people suffers from anxiety.

You bail.

Bailing can be a good thing if it means you recognized some red flags from your relationship and life inventories and you realize this isn't the right guy. Another reason you might bail is if the guy you're with inadvertently triggers a bad memory or a hot button. In this case, you need to start to recognize those hot buttons and assign them to the proper relationship – one in the past.

If, however, you panic and bail with a good guy, you're again allowing your anxiety to kick in. It may be that you're afraid of being hurt again.

No man is good enough.

Part of you wants the intimacy and excitement of a relationship, but part of you is holding back or afraid of a negative. You may be afraid of getting hurt or afraid of getting bored. Maybe you fear losing your independence. Unfortunately for you, the part of you that doesn't want a relationship is more significant than the part of you that does.

You may be conforming to social pressure or the pressure of friends and family to find someone. Rather than admit you simply don't want a relationship, you might be putting it off on him – he was too much of a workaholic; he was too controlling; he was too critical; etc.

Ask yourself what percentage of you does want a relationship. Put it into a percentage. Sit and think about it for a while. Conversely, ask yourself what part of you wants to stay single. That can tell you a lot about whether or not you're ready.

What's Next?

If you find yourself shying away from relationships at this point, it's probably a good time to spend some time reading my confidence book for women, *Comfortable in Your Own Shoes.* This book will take a few of the things you've learned along the way here, and it will take a deeper dive into those topics and others.

If, on the other hand, you find yourself comfortable in dating, go slowly, watch for red flags and trust your gut. You have learned a lot in this journey of healing and now you're going to take all of it for a spin - get the dust off if you will. Don't push yourself, just enjoy the process.

Keep the pressure off to find a relationship and enjoy dating for what it is - meeting lots of new, great men!

Chapter 16

How to Date
in a Healthy Way

Let's think of dating in a new way. Let's go into dating with a healthy outlook and the proper expectations. Healthy dating means having those boundaries in place, knowing where happiness comes from, being confident with high self-esteem and taking things slowly. Let's look at some tips on healthy dating.

Stay Safe!

Of course, this might seem like a no-brainer, but if you have been out of the dating scene for a while, your excitement over getting back out there might make you a little careless at first. Make sure your first few dates with a new man happen in a specific way. Meet in public. Arrange your first meeting at a coffee shop or other brightly lit environment that isn't too noisy.

Meet him at your chosen venue for the first few dates, don't allow him to pick you up at your house. If possible, especially on the first date, arrive early. Also protect your personal phone number. Get a phone number on Google or another similar system and use that for your dates. By the same token, get an alternate email and use that until you get to know him.

Treat A First Date Like A Meeting

First dates are the worst, aren't they? Everyone is on edge, trying to present the best version of themselves. You get your hair and makeup just right. You asked 10 friends about your outfit before you got dressed. What if we treat first dates differently? What if we take the pressure off?

Whether you met your guy online, at the grocery store or through a friend, a first date is a creature of a different color compared to any of those situations. You could talk to someone online for days or weeks and feel a strong connection but when it's time to meet, your nerves are a bundle.

If you treat a first date as a meeting, which is what it truly is, then you begin to alleviate some of the pressure. Looking at the first date as a meeting means you have a different agenda. A first date agenda is the need to impress – the need to make him want a second date. The agenda of a meeting is to learn more about the other person, to see if there are any immediate red flags. When you have a meeting with someone, you're introducing yourself and observing. You are beginning the learning process about this man.

He Needs To Be Good Enough For You!

In your previous dating life, you may have felt the need to be good enough for him but we are turning those tables around. You are a highly confident, high value woman who deserves to be treated well. Rather than worrying about whether or not you are good enough for him, you need to evaluate whether he is good enough for you! Perhaps this is a good time to introduce you to my book, *Weed Out the Users, the Couch Potatoes and the Losers.*

You no longer take any crap from a man. You don't fall for their stall tactics or smooth talking lines. You are a woman who understands that she deserves to be loved by a good man and you won't settle for anything less.

Have Fun – He Is

Men and women go into dating differently. Men find dating fun. They love the chase and they love the mystery and challenge of dating a woman. Women start dating a new guy and immediately start evaluating him to see if he will be a good provider, a good partner.

Date to have fun. Enjoy the process. Do fun things with new men. Try new restaurants and new foods. Explore your new hobbies, if possible, on your dates. Stop trying to eval-uate him as marriage material from date 1 and just enjoy!

Don't Start With The Milestones

I never realized women tallied milestones until it was pointed out to me by a woman. I have told my story a few times of a woman I was seeing who was tallying milestones while I was just enjoying the getting to know her process.

From the first date on, women tend to start tallying mile-stones. He kisses you or he doesn't. He holds your hand or the date goes longer than expected. He asks right away for another date or he calls an hour later. These all count for something in the book of women but to men, it's just dating. It goes back to the having fun discussion we just had. He is having fun and he's not considering that his actions may be mistakenly leading you to believe he's getting more and more serious about you. Trust me, we're clueless about this!

Listen More Than You Speak

This is a hard one because for some people, when they get nervous, they talk more. Try to resist the urge to talk his head off. If you catch yourself talking a lot, smile and say something like, "I'm so sorry, I've been talking the whole time".

Ask him questions. If you met online, you can scan his profile or the email exchanges between you ahead of time and have some questions ready. Don't make him feel like he's being interrogated but say something like, "I saw you like to ski. Where do you like to go?" or "I saw that pic of your cat. He's awesome – what's his name?"

Remain A Secret

What I mean by this is don't spill your entire life story either in emails before you meet or in conversations shortly after. The first date is not the time to tell your entire life story. Aside from that, men love mystery and challenge. He is enjoying not knowing everything about you. It will be partly a challenge to him to learn more and also he wants the mystery to be revealed slowly.

The other side of this coin is that if you spill everything in email before you meet or in the first date or two, you won't have anything to talk about. It makes your subsequent dates very difficult. You've already shared everything. He will quickly determine there is no more mystery and challenge to dating you and he will move on.

No Sex

If you plan to just go out there and seek out a bunch of hookups fine, but otherwise, you make a man earn sex. I mentioned this earlier. This is a boundary you need to put in place. I can't tell you how many dates or how much time you need to wait but I can tell you that it isn't in the first few dates.

He needs to first prove to you that he's interested in you, not just what's in your jeans. Even a good guy will get in your pants if you let him. The difference is that a good guy will then internally label you as a rest stop – a woman he can have sex with, without commitment. If you want him to view you as a keeper – a woman he can marry – then you don't give him sex.

There is another reason for waiting. Once you have sex with a guy, you've lost the ability to determine whether or not he's a good guy. You've leapfrogged over the process of getting to know him. You are invested in a new way, on a new level. Your vision where he is concerned is clouded after you have sex with him.

Note How You Feel After

If you're a journal-writing type of person, this is a good opportunity for you. If not, do this introspectively. Take note of how you feel after the date. Was he who you thought he would be? Does he show any early warning signs, based on your relationship inventory? Did you enjoy his company? Did he make you feel anxious or nervous? Why?

Either write about what you feel or meditate on it or something but truly and carefully consider your real feelings. Do this after the date and then do it again a day or so later, when you're not feeling the high of meeting someone new. Is he like the men of your past? How? In the positive or negative traits? It is important for you to recognize your feelings and act accordingly. If you saw red flags, don't cover them up with excuses. Move on.

Go Slowly

If you do like this guy, move slowly. Meet and go somewhere a few times. Just enjoy yourself. Don't move in right away, don't sleep together right away. Allow yourself to experience the exhilaration of romantic love without pushing too hard. If it's meant to be, it will happen naturally.

Allow him to chase you. Keep the mystery alive by not sharing too much. Challenge him by changing things up. If you normally show up for a date wearing a skirt and blouse, try jeans and a comfy shirt. If you normally wear your hair up, let it down. If you usually order a mojito, get something else you like. Anticipate his movements and be ahead of him. If he usually orders a specific type of beer, have one waiting for him. This will get easier every time and you won't be able to anticipate his movements early on so don't sweat that one until you've known him longer.

Don't Cave On Your Boundaries Or Values

If you aren't ready for sex but he's pushing you to go for it anyway, stand your ground. You can simply tell him you want to move slowly and if he isn't okay with that, maybe you should stop seeing one another. Sometimes this is all a guy needs to back off but if he doesn't, get out your big sign that says "NEXT!"

You should never give up on your boundaries or change your values for someone else. If you change, it needs to be because you're making a choice to do so for your own reasons, not because someone else is pushing you to do so. There are more men out there, men who will respect your boundaries and who will love you for your values.

Don't Make Snap Judgments

People often make a judgement after a first date about whether or not they want to continue dating someone. I encourage you not to do this. Unless this guy shows some real red flags, give him a few dates to get to know you and you him.

Of course, if he shows himself to be a real jerk, you don't need to keep dating him, but if it's just a matter of not feeling anything, give it time. True feelings of love take time. If you would like to watch me discuss this topic with some female dating experts and Dr. Helen Fisher, click here: www.whoholdsthecardsnow.com/yourtango-the-experts-why-do-men-get-spooked/.

Stay In The Present

Resist the female urge to look into the future, especially early on. Don't start thinking marriage right away. Don't let your imagination run wild with thoughts of a house, picket fence, minivan and 3 kids. Stay in the moment. Stay present in where your relationship is right now.

Don't Take Rejection Personally

If the first meeting doesn't go well, write it off as a nice evening. Don't take it personally. If he doesn't contact you back, that's okay. It isn't that you're a bad person, it's that you're not a good fit for him. The same goes for you. You don't owe him an explanation and you don't need to feel guilty if you don't like him or want to see him again. Just thank him for an enjoyable time and move on.

By the same token, if you're talking to someone online and he disappears, he probably met someone he's more interested in. He didn't stop communicating because he thought you were too fat, too thin, or too anything. He simply moved on. He doesn't owe you an explanation, especially in the world of online dating. Don't rip off a bunch of snarky, nasty emails. Just accept you weren't his type and keep looking.

Don't Berate Yourself

Just because a date doesn't go well doesn't mean you're a loser. I know your self-esteem is a little fragile right now – it's fresh and new. A bad date doesn't mean the end of the world. Turn it into a funny story to tell your friends. Don't take this too seriously. It was just a meeting with a man. It is just one evening with one man.

The worst thing to happen is you wasted a few hours. Tell yourself you're fine. Nothing is wrong with you. You need to keep repeating that to yourself. Reject your rejector. If he shot you down that quickly, he wasn't worth your time anyway.

If Dating Throws You Back Into Grieving

Early on in your dating, you may find yourself grieving the old relationship again. You may see or smell something which reminds you of your ex. You may hear a song or your new guy may dress similarly. Any number of things could trigger your grief.

Back off of dating for a little while and allow yourself to feel the grief. Set a time limit for it, though and don't allow yourself to be dragged down by it. As before, do not allow yourself to stuff the feelings, feel the pain but do not allow yourself to stay in that negative space.

Use this as a gauge to see what it is you may still need to work on. Go back and redo lessons you feel you need to repeat. This is not a bad thing. It's a good thing because you get more time to work on yourself before Mr. Right steps into your life. By then, you will be ready!

Chapter 17

Wrap Up

I have thrown a lot at you in this book and in your first read-through, it may seem overwhelming. Remember, though, that you don't need to do all of the activities as you come to them. Do them when you feel you're ready. Some of them will be more helpful than others. Some might make you feel uncomfortable, which may make you want to shy away from completing the exercises. In that instance, you need to push through and feel the uncomfortable feelings. This will help you get more comfortable feeling things you aren't accustomed to feeling.

You may have been a feeling stuffer in the past and you've got a lot of pain now, piled onto what you've stuffed previously. It is my goal to keep you from stuffing these feelings. That is counterproductive to your healing and I want you to achieve a full recovery! It is important for you to feel the pain, to feel the anxiety and recognize that it does pass and that the pain will lessen with time, when you allow yourself to feel it. When you stuff it, it only grows.

Your recovery will take time. I don't know which phase of the grieving process you're experiencing right now, so I cannot predict how long you will feel as crappy as you did when you bought this book but what I do know is that, if you do the work here, you will feel better. This will begin to feel survivable! Remember, I have told you numerous times throughout this book that your recovery should go at your pace, not someone else's. Don't let others encourage you to take steps you're not ready for. Don't allow someone to belittle what you're feeling.

Kindly remind people that this is your grieving and you are different than they are. You need to proceed through this healing at your pace and you would appreciate their support. They are your friends and family and they do mean well – they hurt when they see you hurt.

The only other point I want to drive home right now is that it is imperative to your healing that you put into place and enforce the no contact rule. You must do this for yourself. Many of the steps in this book are not meant to harm the other people in your life, but they are intended to help you move forward in a healthy way and that is my goal. I am concerned about you and your healing! Remember the free resources I have provided – you have one free book to download and I am listing the remainder of my books at the end of this book. My books cost less than the cost of a cup of coffee and they are easy and quick to read.

Author Bio

As one of Boston's top dating coaches, my books rest prominently atop the dating advice genre. In my role as a life coach, I've been known to be unorthodox, in a good way, and I break a few rules. I assist both men and women and help them understand one another.

I won't bore you with my professional bio. Instead, I will share with you the story of how I became a dating and life coach and what makes me qualified to coach you.

The irony of my story is that I come from an extremely dysfunctional family. I witnessed the marriage of my parents crumble before my eyes at an early age. Flying dishes seemed normal in my household. I came out a bit angry and I have 12 years of failed relationships to show for it.

Fortunately, I started encountering positive things in my life. I discovered that couple, that elusive, elderly couple still holding hands in the park at the ripe old age of eighty. They gave me hope. As a problem solver, I could solve anything…except relationships, damn it!

I couldn't figure out why my folks represented the norm rather than the exception to married life. Fifty-five percent of all marriages end in divorce. Why? "What is wrong?"

In 2009, after a long stretch of living the single life, I had an epiphany. I attended a Christmas show at my Dad's church. I am not a religious person, but when I saw the cheerful couples and witnessed the powerful music, I was touched. I needed answers to love and I wanted true love for myself.

I was tired of my shallow single life. I decided to study my failures and interview as many single people and couples as I could. I even watched the movie, Hitch, and it motivated me to help others.

I realized I possessed a natural ability to help others discover love, and knew it was my future. Can you guess where I started? Yep, those happy elderly couples. Sure, I got maced a few times as I approached them with questions, but the knowledge I gained was priceless!

Since then, I have met thousands of people: happy couples, unhappy couples, single people of all types, and everything in between. I quickly learned that confidence played a large role in both attracting and keeping a partner.

My friends encouraged me to launch a dating advice website. I now own the top dating site for women, Who Holds the Cards Now.

Men and women contact me after reading my books. I have become a "Dear Abby" of sorts. Today, after thousands of interviews, I have accomplished my goal. I broke the code and enjoy a great relationship myself. Now I plan to share my findings with **you**!

I have come to realize that even though people believe what I teach, they still suffer a serious problem. They lack the motivation and confidence to execute my tactics. A course change was required. I started concentrating on life coaching in addition to my date coaching. If you can't love yourself, how can you love someone else? It's impossible.

Now, I concentrate on pulling people in and guiding them to understanding themselves. I assist them in creating clarity in their lives, setting goals, and creating the path to attain those goals. I offer inspiration, passion, and spirituality with the constant live like you're dying attitude. People are transformed through my books and daily exercises.

I have written 15 Amazon Best Sellers, four of which reached #1 Best Seller status. Together we can build your confidence, increase your self-esteem, and propel you closer to your goals.

You will discover happiness by completing the work most people will never attempt!

Today, I travel and teach in all the sexy playgrounds: LA, South Beach, and Las Vegas. I can help you in your journey to find love and build confidence so we can transform your life.

I am not merely a best-selling author, my readers are my friends and I communicate with them directly. I humbly ask you to allow me to help you. Join me on my quest for your happiness, your exciting journey to an extraordinary life!

Gregg Michaelsen, Confidence Builder

I feel you need two very important skills before you start dating again: confidence in yourself and an understanding of the male mind. I provide both because I am a life coach and a male dating coach. I have two rockin' paid courses with tons of videos featuring me if you're interested.

Understand men here: www.whoholdsthecardsnow. com/product/the-man-whisperer/

Find confidence here: www.whoholdsthecardsnow. com/product/build-will-come/

Get the Word Out to Your Friends

If you believe your friends would draw something valuable from this book, I'd be honored if you'd share your thoughts with them. If you feel particularly strong about the contributions this book made to your success, I'd be eternally grateful if you would post a review on Amazon. You can check them out by clicking the links below. My coed motivational books are listed after the women's books.

Women's Dating Advice Books

Please read the jewel of all my books: *To Date a Man, You Must Understand a Man*. This companion book to all my books will help you understand men! Read the hundreds and hundreds of reviews to learn how well my tactics work! Another #1 best seller.

Next, take understanding men to another level with *10 Secrets You Need to Know About Men*.

If you want to make sure you don't get played, you need to read *Weed Out The Users, The Couch Potatoes and the Losers*.

One of my latest books is selling like crazy! *Pennies in the Jar: How to Keep a Man for Life* is the ultimate women's guide to keeping a relationship strong!

More Awesome Best Sellers to Solve Your Dating Issues!

Would you like to make a man fall in love with you?
Try *Night Moves*!

If you're single and looking? Read *The Social Tigress*.

When you can't stand the thought of picking up one
more player, you need to read *Weed Out the Losers,
The Couch Potatoes and The Losers*.

Do you want to learn more about men?
Read *Manimals: Understanding Different Types of Men
and How to Date Them*.

Are you ready for a serious change?
Read *Own Your Tomorrow*.

Do you want to text a man into submission?
#1 Best Seller: *Power Texting Men*.

Would you like to take yourself on a self-discovery journey?
Read *To Date a Man You Must Understand Yourself*.

Do you want your ex back? I'll give you your best
chance with *How to Get Your Ex Back Fast*.

If you want to regain control of your relationship,
try *Who Holds the Cards Now?*

Confidence attracts!
Get it here: <u>Comfortable in Your Own Shoes</u>.

Would you like to clean up online?
Read *Love is in The Mouse* and *Love is in the Mouse 2017*.

Are you over 40 and getting back into the dating scene?
Check out *Middle Aged and Kickin' It*.

Are you in need of some introvert dating help?
Take a peek at *Be Quiet and Date Me!*.

And, last but not least, for the long distance couple:
Committed to Love, Separated by Distance.

Books for Men and Women that Motivate!

Live Like You're Dying

The Power to Communicate

I can be reached at Gregg@WhoHoldsTheCardsNow.com.

Please visit my website just for women,
WhoHoldstheCardsNow.com.

Facebook: WhoHoldsTheCardsNow
Twitter: @YouHoldTheCards
I'm a Your Tango Expert

You are my motivation!
Gregg